BROOKLYN

The Way It Was

OVER 200 VINTAGE PHOTOGRAPHS

FROM THE

COLLECTION OF BRIAN MERLIS

Israelowitz Publishing

P.O.Box 228 Brooklyn, NY 11229

Tel. (718) 951-7072   FAX (718) 951-7072

This book is dedicated to the loving memory of Rose Merlis.

Contents

Atlas of Long Island, 1873, Beers, Comstock & Cline

Introduction

By definition, *nostalgia* is a yearning for the past, in part, a recalling of our physical roots, bringing to mind indelible recollections of our youth, whether they be "golden" or not. To me, growing up in Brooklyn was the *raison d'être* of *Welcome Back to Brooklyn*. In response to the overwhelming reception that it has already received, I have authored *Brooklyn–The Way It Was*. This sequel, much greater in scope than its initial volume, attempts to document a panoramic overview of Kings County, as it evolved from its status as several independent political entities prior to 1898, to its present role as New York City's most populous borough. I have placed an emphasis upon the history of the original villages and townships, their precise borders and their growth into today's loosely-defined residential neighborhoods of ever-changing demographics. Every effort has been made to give the reader exact locations of each photograph in the book. Access to dozens of rare and early street atlases and directories has made this arduous task possible. In this, my most ambitious undertaking, I have attempted to present a pictorial history that would be of interest to the uninitiated as well as stand the test of critical review.

It is hoped that a representative selection of meaningful street scenes have been included. It is doubtful that it could be all that one could hope for. In chronicling an exciting century in its past, it has been my objective to capture the flavor of the Brooklyn you grew up in or heard so much about. I have endeavored to recast the borough in a new light, that it might lead to a greater respect for the past we all long to revisit.

BM

Acknowledgments

Brooklyn - The Way It Was could not have been produced without the help of the following institutions and individuals: William Asadorian, Charles Young and George Miller of the Queens Borough Public Library, Long Island Division; Claire Lamers at the Brooklyn Historical Society; I. Stephen Miller and the Sheepshead Bay Historical Society; Ray and Elsie Oberg and Ira Kluger of the Canarsie Historical Society; Lucille Posner of the Boro Park Historical Society; members of the Long Island Post Card, especially Charles Huttunen and Ray DiMaria; members of the Metropolitan Post Card Club, notably Leah Schnall; Allen Kent of Bath Beach for his true friendship as well as access to his pictures; Ken Brady of Port Jefferson for his inspiration and patronage; Bob and Helene Stonehill of Jackson Heights for their patience and support; Howard Rose of Gravesend for his friendship and advice; Charles Shapiro of Sheepshead Bay for his fair dealing and integrity; Ron Marzlock of Kew Gardens for his phenomenal abilities; Joel Streich of Commack for his consideration; Tom Sarro of Dyker Heights for keeping me in mind; David Galinsky of Midwood for his unending generosity, Vincent F. Seyfried of Garden City for his example of humility: Joe Trapani of Baldwin for his friendship; Greg Campolo of Dyker Heights for paying the tolls to Staten Island and New Jersey; Ron Schweiger of Flatlands for his terrific slide shows and love of Brooklyn's history; Bob and Ginger Wexler of Tourneau for their hospitality; and Paul Brigandi of Greenlawn for our recent association. Appreciation also goes to newcomers Sal Dono of Flatbush, Lee Rosenzweig of Flatlands, Mike Schaum of Belle Harbor, Ken Kimmel of Gravesend and Neil Terens of Sheepshead Bay. Thanks to all my co-workers at Canarsie High School, especially to assistant editor Steve Brown. A special thanks goes to Rita and Jack Merlis, who reviewed the final draft and came up with the perfect title. Gratitude is due to Oscar Israelowitz, who designed the excellent layout for this book. To my kids, Heather and Joshua, and my wife, Debbie, thanks for your loving support in this project.

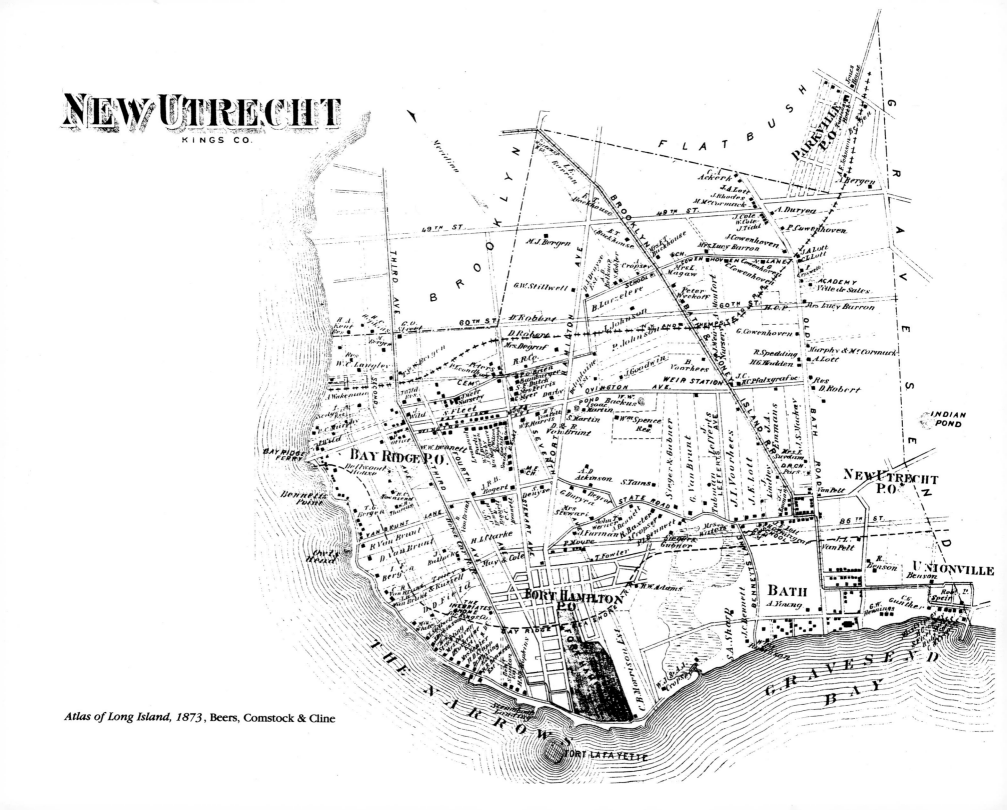

NEW UTRECHT

KINGS CO.

Atlas of Long Island, 1873, Beers, Comstock & Cline

Bath Beach

All of Bath Beach and most of Bensonhurst were part of the Town of New Utrecht until annexation in 1894. The old Village of New Utrecht, centered near 18th Avenue and 84th Street, was given the name *Van Pelt Manor* in 1890 by real estate developers. 84th Street, from 16th to 18th Avenues was part of the original Kings Highway and was the village's Main Street for over two hundred years.

Settled in 1657 by the Dutch, the town was named after *Utrecht*, a city in Holland. Families named Backer, Cortelyou, de Sille and Van Brunt were among the town's first settlers. New Utrecht was chartered in 1661. The governor ordered it to be barricaded to protect the settlement from attacks by the indigenous population. Most of the village had to be rebuilt after the fire of 1675. On August 25, 1776, the Second Brigade of Hessians under the command of Lt. General de Heister landed at Bath (Beach).

By the early 1800s the waterfront area had become a popular bayside resort. It managed to survive until the late 1930s at which time the old bath houses and dance halls were taken down to make way for the Belt Parkway. A few of the old villas still can be found in the area, some along Bay 11th Street. Other old houses remain on Benson, Bath and 18th Avenues, vestiges of better days now past.

Bensonhurst was developed as Bensonhurst-by-the-Sea on lands belonging to the Benson family. Lots were sold as early as 1888. Large wood-frame homes were constructed on and contiguous to Bay Parkway. The development spread across the old town line and extended into what was formerly Gravesend, east of Stillwell Avenue near Kings Highway. An attractive park along Gravesend Bay was built for the area's residents. Today, Bensonhurst is blocked off from the water by the Belt Parkway.

Development of Bath Beach-Bensonhurst was facilitated by the area's proximity to the Brooklyn, Bath and Coney Island Rail Road, which provided transportation to Coney Island and to points north. Many of the old homes have been removed over the last 50 years so that new houses could replace them. Apartment houses were built on large lots that were available after the older homes were demolished.

Today, the area has become the domicile for recent immigrants from the former Soviet Union and Italy. "Old timers," which include second- and third-generation Jews and Italians still make their homes in Bensonhurst. A growing number of Asians, Latinos and African-Americans have recently come to the area as well.

Bath Avenue, looking southeast from Bay 19th Street, 1920

Steel rails from the BRT along Bath Avenue connect with the tracks of the Brooklyn, Bath & West End Rail Road at left. That company was founded in 1862 and within five years became the first rail link to Coney Island. The road was electrified in 1899-1900. The right-of-way continued to be used by trolley cars from 1916 until the late 1940s, utilizing New Utrecht Avenue and Bay 19th Street in addition to Bath Avenue.

De Bruyn's Lane, looking southwest from Cropsey Avenue toward Gravesend Bay, 1922

De Bruyn's Lane began at the Kings Highway, near to what is now 21st Avenue and 81st Street. Known also as the Old Bath Road, it ran between 20th Avenue and Bay 23rd Street until it reached the water. A remnant of it may be seen today where it crossed Bath Avenue.

16th Avenue, looking northeast from Bath to Benson Avenues, 1919

16th Avenue was still unpaved at this time. Trolley tracks along Bath Avenue are visible in the foreground. The building in the distance is on the corner of Benson Avenue.

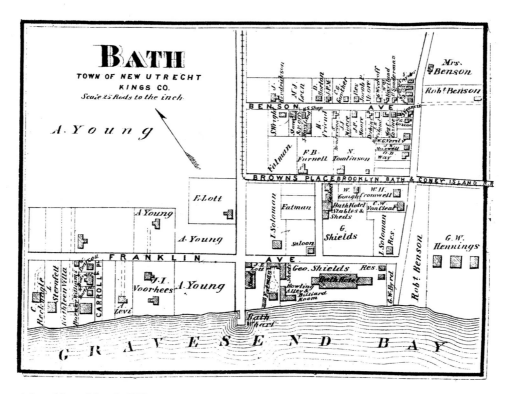

Atlas of Long Island, 1873. Beers, Comstock & Cline

**Graduating Class of Public School No. 163 -
Benson Avenue at Bay 14th Street, ca. 1912**

This brick school building opened its doors in 1910. These students may have been members of the school's first graduating class. The Horton's (ice cream) sign at right is on No. 1653 Benson Avenue.

18th Avenue, looking northeast at Benson Avenue, 1929

This busy scene, taken from the entrance of John Licht's store, shows the diversity of businesses along the avenue. On the right side are a Chevrolet service station, the Bath Beach Poultry Market, the Mashin Lumber Company, an "auto laundry" and Engine Company No. 243. In the distance, a section of the West End elevated line is faintly visible.

18th Avenue, looking southwest from Benson Avenue, 1929

John Licht's automobile electrical establishment was located at No. 8696 18th Avenue. The roadway was paved with cobblestones which are smaller and more uniform than Belgian blocks.

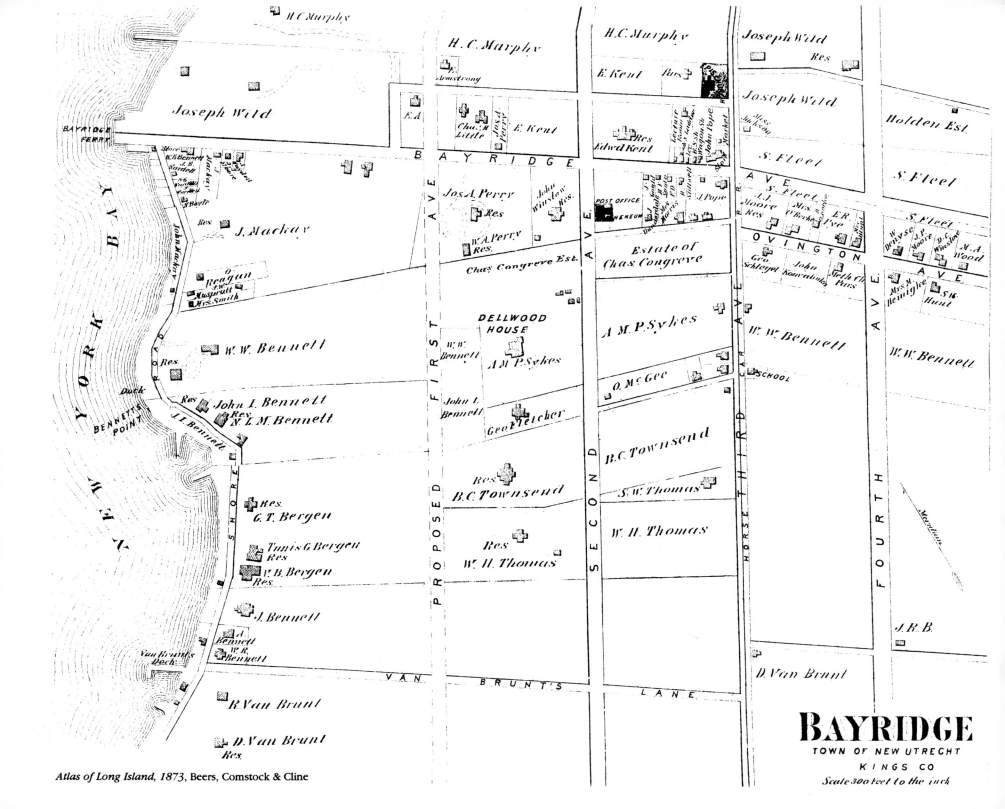

Atlas of Long Island, 1873, Beers, Comstock & Cline

BAYRIDGE
TOWN OF NEW UTRECHT
KINGS CO
Scale 300 feet to the inch

Bay Ridge

Located on the westernmost lands of Long Island, Bay Ridge and Fort Hamilton were, until 1894, part of the Town of New Utrecht. In 1524, Giovanni da Verrazzano landed at this site when he sailed into New York Bay. It wasn't until 1652 that the *Nyack Tract*, which included lands near the Narrows, was purchased by Cornelius Van Werckhoven.

During the American Revolution, the British landed at Denyse's Ferry on August 22, 1776. Shells from battleships damaged homes belonging to the Bennetts and the Denyses. In 1807, a military defense was installed at the Narrows. The cornerstone was laid in 1825, and by 1831 the 96-acre reservation at Fort Hamilton was completed. A young captain named Robert E. Lee as well as Stonewall Jackson were stationed at Fort Hamilton prior to the Civil War.

Fort Diamond, located on a small island offshore, was renamed Fort Lafayette when the Frenchman visited Brooklyn in 1825. The island was later used as the foundation for the Brooklyn tower of the Verrazzano-Narrows Bridge.

Bay Ridge was called "Yellow Hook" until 1854. Citizens changed the name because a Yellow Fever epidemic gave the town a negative connotation. Wealthy individuals built mansions along Shore Road during the late 1800s. Pioneer families such as the Bergens and the Van Brunts slowly sold off their farms and estates soon after the town's annexation.

Private clubs like the Crescent Athletic Club served the social needs of the area's elite. As land further away from the shore was sold around the turn of the century, middle-class families were able to move into the neighborhood. Germans, Irish and Scandinavians began to move in. Some came from the densely populated areas in the former City of Brooklyn.

The area near Fort Hamilton still has houses dating from the early to mid-1800s. As the 20th century progressed, Italians, followed by Greeks, moved into the section. By World War I, the Roman Catholic population of the area had grown considerably, although the Lutheran sect predominated.

The BMT subway reached Bay Ridge via 4th Avenue by 1916. Apartment houses were constructed along Ridge Boulevard and the avenues, beginning in the 1920s. Many elegant homes of yesteryear were torn down as the value of Bay Ridge property increased. In 1964, a great suspension bridge linking Staten and Long Islands was completed. Today, Bay Ridge-Fort Hamilton is a cultural melting pot where traditional family values have kept the area a desirable place to live.

Shore Road, looking north from 85th Street, 1906

The hedges on the right border the 10-acre grounds of the Crescent Athletic Club which was destroyed by fire in the 1930s. Fort Hamilton High School now stands on this site. The beautiful building on the left was the club's boat house. It too is no longer extant.

Bliss Estate, as seen from Shore Road, 1906

E.W. Bliss was born at Cooperstown, NY in 1836. By the age of 23 he managed the Charles Parker Gun Company of Meriden, CT. After seeing action at Bull Run during the Civil War, he linked up with Charles Pratt and Frederick W. Devoe, who were prominent in the oil industry. Bliss moved to Brooklyn in 1866, where he invented and secured patents for torpedoes and other projectiles.

As he became more successful, he purchased the Henry C. Murphy estate with additional lands totaling 65 acres, at Bay Ridge. He erected an observatory tower of granite at a cost of $16,000. Although the tower and mansion are gone today, part of the property is preserved as Owl's Head Park, which became public in the 1920s.

**Fourth Avenue,
looking north from 95th Street, 1918 (opposite)**
This funeral procession during World War I originated at
Fort Hamilton and proceeded along Fourth Avenue toward
Green-Wood Cemetery, a distance of about three miles.
The larger building fronts Fifth Avenue to the far right.

**RKO Dyker Theatre
- No. 525 86th Street, early 1970s (opposite)**

This motion picture theatre was built in the 1920s. It closed shortly after this photograph was taken.

Nos. 442-420 89th Street, between Fourth and Fifth Avenues, 1930

89th Street was called Waverly Place until New Utrecht was annexed in 1894. These wood-frame houses, built prior to the Civil War, served as residences for immigrants in the 19th century. Structures of this age still exist in the neighborhood.

**Fifth Avenue,
looking north toward 89th Street, 1930**

Much of the area south of 86th Street escaped the changes brought about by the building boom of the 1920s. As a result, those blocks retained the character and ambiance of an earlier period.

Bedford-Stuyvesant

Bedford-Stuyvesant, a large district which lies between Crown Heights, Bushwick, Williamsburg and Clinton Hill, comprised approximately three wards in the old City of Brooklyn. Its name is derived from two nineteenth-century communities. Bedford was a colonial hamlet situated in the vicinity of Fulton Street and Bedford Avenue. Stuyvesant Heights was a name given by developers to the area near MacDonough Street, extending from Tompkins to Stuyvesant Avenues.

In the 1830s the area was the site of two African-American communities, Weeksville and Carrville. By 1885, most of the 600 African-Americans had been displaced. They left small, wood-frame homes, a church, school and orphanage. Weeksville was located near Atlantic Avenue, at the old Hunterfly Road, near the border of Crown Heights.

In 1875, the area witnessed phenomenal growth. For twenty years, magnificent row houses, rivaling those anywhere in Brooklyn, were constructed of brick and brownstone. Many of these buildings were accentuated with terra cotta and stained glass windows. Some ornate apartment houses were built prior to 1900. The area had become one of the city's best, and attracted well-to-do families and upwardly mobile working-class people.

The completion of the Independent "A" train in 1936 provided a direct connection from Harlem to Bedford-Stuyvesant. Many native-born African-Americans had come to Harlem during the great migration of the 1920s. Thousands fled the intimidation and death threats made by racist groups in the south, and soon found themselves in Brooklyn. During the Great Depression, many of the homes in Bedford-Stuyvesant were subdivided into multi-family dwellings in order to meet the increased demand for housing. An influx of West Indian people in the 1920s slightly altered the demography of the area.

Whites began selling, and the increased population density caused slum conditions to develop in certain parts of the area. At least one block association was formed to discourage home sales to Blacks, and a Ku Klux Klan chapter found some support in the section. But, aside from a few instances of racial friction, the transition of Bedford-Stuyvesant proceeded smoothly, and numerous instances of community and church cooperation between groups are a matter of record. By the early 1960s, most of the Whites had moved away from Bedford-Stuyvesant.

One of the neighborhood's architectural gems is Boys' High School, located at No. 832 Marcy Avenue. It was designed by James W. Haughton and was built in 1891. Much of the area remains architecturally intact.

While a few old-timers of European descent remain there to this day, Bedford-Stuyvesant is mainly inhabited by African-Americans who take pride in their homes, churches and community heritage dating back to the 1830s.

Northeast corner Gates and Clinton Avenues, 1899

The old Slocum house, built prior to the Civil War, had just been sold. That building, as well as the house to its north, were soon to be demolished to make way for brick homes. Today, they are included in the Clinton Hill Historic District.

Engine No. 230 - No. 59 Ellery Street, (opposite) between Marcy and Nostrand Avenues, 1922

1922 marked the last year that horse-drawn engines were used in Brooklyn. Their demise began in 1908 when, at its height, the department used 804 fire horses. This company was moved to a new location, No. 701 Park Avenue, around 1960.

Lewis Avenue, looking north at Decatur Street, 1929

Public School No. 35 is at left, on the northwest corner. Today's Stuyvesant Heights Historic District includes the buildings on the far right. Note the luncheonette on the corner featuring Reid's ice cream.

Fulton Street, looking west from Lewis Avenue, 1956
Chauncey Street is at right. Vestigial trolley tracks are visible at left.

**Vacation School -
Public School No. 45 at Lafayette and Classon Avenues, 1902**

Vacation playgrounds provided recreational activities for Brooklyn's children during the hot summer months. This service was instituted as an outgrowth of the Progressive Era, which increased social services nationwide.

Fulton Street grocery, ca. 1914

Linden Dairy, ca. 1905

Women had to bring their pre-school children to the shop.

**H.L. Ennis, Decorations
- southwest corner of Gates and Nostrand
Avenues, 1900 (opposite)**

This site would soon be cleared to allow for the
construction of the Long Island Storage Warehouse, built
around 1910. The warehouse appears on this page.

30897

86th Street and Bay Parkway, looking toward Bath Beach, 1918

This beautiful home was built around 1890 in the development of Bensonhurst-by-the-Sea. It was razed in 1920 to allow for the commercial development of 86th Street.

Bath Avenue, looking northwest toward Bay Parkway, 1921

What is now a busy intersection was then a quiet crossroads. As the years passed, the neighborhood became more developed and the small town atmosphere vanished.

79th Street, looking northwest toward 21st Avenue, 1925

The 1870s' farmhouse and barn at No. 2103 79th Street were owned by Philip Pfalzgraf who farmed almost 20 acres here. A defunct portion of Kings Highway is visible where the curb is absent. The road extended to the far right of the photograph and continued to Bay Parkway, where it begins today. A fence has been built around the lot where several stucco homes would soon be built.

86th Street, looking northwest toward Bay 26th Street, 1918 (opposite)

This famous shopping district replaced Bath Avenue as the principal thoroughfare when the West End elevated line was constructed in 1916. Three-story brick commercial buildings, with apartments upstairs, were first erected on the odd-numbered side of 86th Street about 1910. The opposite side of the street retained its residential character until the boom of the 1920s, when two-story brick structures began replacing the existing frame houses. Note the gas street lamp left over from an earlier era.

Bergen Beach, looking north along boardwalk near Avenue Y and East 74th Street, 1923

Begun in the 1890s, this resort was reached via the Flatbush Avenue streetcar, which turned east onto Avenue N. The heyday of the Bergen Beach resort had come to an end after World War I. The boardwalk and the attractions had fallen into disrepair. The casino at right, as well as all of the remaining structures, were eventually razed to make way for the Belt Parkway.

Bergen Beach

**No. 7071 Avenue V,
northwest corner of East 71st Street, 1926**

Built in the 1890s, this large home probably became the oldest house in Bergen Beach after the Bergen House was demolished around 1930. This view is looking west along Avenue V.

Stoothoff - Bergen House, south side of Avenue V, between East 72nd and East 73rd Streets, 1924

Bergen Beach was one of the many islands in Jamaica Bay before the inlet was filled in around 1895. In the early 1600s it was known as Mentelaer's Island. According to scholars, it was built by the Dutch West India Company as a trading post in 1656 and was altered and enlarged over the decades. Bergen Beach was a summer resort from 1895 to 1920. The Bergen House was used as a hotel but was razed after the resort's demise.

Borough Park

Situated in the Town of New Utrecht until 1894, this section remained rural farmland until the development of Blythebourne in 1886. Electus B. Litchfield, son of Edwin C. Litchfield of Prospect Park fame, bought some vacant land west of New Utrecht Avenue, from about 57th to about 53rd Street. He named the area Blythebourne, which means "Happy Home." In order to develop the area, he opened a real estate office at 43rd Street and New Utrecht Avenue. He called it the West Brooklyn Land & Improvement Company of Blythebourne, Long Island. Houses were built and a post office and stores were opened.

For some years, both sides of New Utrecht Avenue were called Blythebourne, but around 1898 Senator William H. Reynolds came and bought land abutting on the east side of the avenue, calling it Borough Park. This tract extended from 43rd to about 60th Streets. The Senator sold lots and also built and sold several two-family houses. Soon, for the use of the people in the two growing communities, he had a large club house erected at 13th Avenue and 50th Street. This was a boon to the neighborhood and many a social affair was held there.

A real estate agent at the time warned the Litchfield family to sell its holdings, explaining that the "pogroms" in Eastern Europe would soon cause a mass migration of Jews into the area and ultimately would bring the land values down. Mrs. William B. Litchfield, who controlled the property at the time, decided not to sell. The prediction was partially fulfilled. The Borough Park section did become a major Jewish community, but the land values, instead of falling, rose tremendously.

On June 6, 1916, the West End "El" opened. The Brooklyn Rapid Transit (BRT) charged only a single five-cent fare for the entire route which extended from Coney Island through Borough Park and to Manhattan. A realty boon was predicted for Borough Park. The *Brooklyn Daily Eagle's* real estate section described the neighborhood in the following article...

"One of the oldest and most historical localities in Brooklyn, Borough Park is particularly favored in natural advantages being supplied with beautiful trees in abundance. It is one of the highest spots in the borough, and is developed from farmland that supplied the people of old Brooklyn with vegetables and fruit. Some of the farms date back to the early Dutch settlers, bearing such names as Van Kouwenhoven, Lefferts and Van Nuyse. The soil of this locality was famous for its productiveness, and many farms reaped substantial fortunes in the days when New Utrecht Avenue was a plank road over which ran Mayor Gunther's steam railroad, a single track line running from Fifth Avenue and 25th Street to Coney Island.

"Modern buildings of every type may be found in the district. The detached, semi-detached, one and two-family and apartment houses in Borough Park compare with the best designs to be found in the city. They have been built in abundance and are located convenient to transit lines. The demand for houses there is increasing every day."

OLDEST HOUSE IN BOROUGH PARK.
LINDEN HEIGHTS, 44TH STREET.

PUBL BY
THE LINDEN PHARMACY
BOROUGH PARK

Stewart McDougall Farm
- looking north from New Utrecht Avenue, ca. 1910

This property once belonged to Adrian Martense. These buildings in this view were located at today's Tenth Avenue, between 44th and 45th Streets. They were razed in the 1910s. This section of Borough Park was known as Linden Heights. All that remains of that namesake is the Linden Heights Jewish Center.

Fort Hamilton Avenue Station, Borough Park, Brooklyn, N. Y.

37th Street, looking southeast from Fort Hamilton Parkway, 1910

The BRT right-of-way continued to run parallel to 37th Street until it reached Gravesend (McDonald) Avenue. The building at right is No. 3709 Fort Hamilton Parkway. An elevated structure was later erected along this right-of-way. It was dismantled in the mid-1980s.

Locomotive May C. of the Brooklyn, Bath & West End Rail Road, ca. 1890
This steam-powered train chugged along New Utrecht and Bath Avenues on its scenic trip to Coney Island.

New Utrecht Avenue, looking north toward 48th Street, 1917

Light struggles to enter between the West End elevated line and the buildings. Smith Brothers' Electric Shoe Repair Shop was located at No. 4820 New Utrecht Avenue.

The Windsor Theatre
- No. 1405 15th Avenue, 1933 (opposite)

Built in the 1920s on the southeast corner of 40th Street, this theatre brought the "Golden Age of Cinema" to Brooklynites. Note the NRA (National Recovery Act) eagle above the entrance.

Brooklyn Navy Yard

**Launching of the
U.S.S. North Carolina, April 9, 1941**
Since the Civil War, the Brooklyn Navy Yard has played an instrumental role in preparing our maritime forces for battle.

Navy Day at the Brooklyn Navy Yard, 1930 (opposite)
The public was invited to examine the facility on October 27, 1930. The smokestacks at left belong to the electric utility.

Brownsville

Brownsville was named for Charles S. and Harrieta C. Brown. In the early 1860s the Vermont couple purchased and subdivided 30 acres. They paid $1200 for the land lying between what is now Rockaway, Blake and Sutter Avenues, and Chester Street. The tract was situated in the northwestern section of the Town of New Lots.

Although hard times delayed swift growth of this new village, by 1874 there were about 150 frame cottages, occupied by Irish, Scottish and a few German families. By 1887, when the Town of New Lots became Brooklyn's 26th Ward, Brownsville had about 4,000 residents living in the approximately 500 homes west of Rockaway Avenue. It was about that time that large numbers of Eastern European Jews began coming to the area. The completion of the Williamsburg Bridge in 1903 added momentum to the flow of Jews into Brownsville.

By 1925, Brownsville and East New York were home to 285,000 Jews, surpassing their number in the Lower East Side of Manhattan. The neighborhood had become the most populous Jewish section in the hemisphere. The area boasted some 70 Orthodox synagogues. A first-class shopping district had been established along Pitkin Avenue by this time.

Brownsville gained nationwide notoriety during the 1940s as the base of operation for an organized crime syndicate known as Murder, Incorporated. The group killed for money by prearranged contract and was also involved in rackets such as gambling, prostitution and extortion of businesses and labor unions.

By the 1950s, many of the residents began to leave and by the mid-1960s the neighborhood's demography had drastically shifted. Today, Brownsville is inhabited mainly by African-Americans and Latinos.

Pushcart Market - North side of Belmont Avenue, looking east from Thatford Avenue, toward Osborn Street, 1955   (opposite)

A mostly Jewish clientele patronizes the businesses in the market. Altman's Drapery, Zwickel's Housewares and Goldstein's Gift Shop all seem to be doing well. Max Slavin & Sons Fish Market still operates their wholesale business out of the same Belmont Avenue location, where they started about 70 years ago.

West Side of Rockaway Avenue near Glenmore Avenue, 1917

Brownsville was one of the world's largest Jewish ghettos. The Canarsie trolley is stalled in front of Okun's Kosher Poultry, at No. 386 Rockaway Avenue, while a boy with his bicycle proudly poses for the photographer.

West Side of Thatford Avenue, looking north toward Dumont Avenue, 1928

Note the architectural details on the wooden porches and terraces on these late 19th century homes.

Blake Avenue, looking east from East 98th Street toward Union Street, 1927.

All of the buildings were erected around 1925. In the distance are Tapscott Street and Howard Avenue. Union Street runs north and south at this point. This part of Brownsville was once within the boundaries of Flatbush.

Sally Argento, Mover - No. 286 Sackman Street near Pitkin Avenue, 1928

Although Brownsville is famous for its Jewish population, a large number of Italian families resided there as well. Here, Salvatore Argento sits proudly in his handsome moving van on a Brownsville street. He and his wife Angelina lived on Sackman Street for many years.

East New York Avenue, looking west at Powell Street, 1919

East New York Avenue was once a plank road which went from the village of Flatbush to the Brooklyn & Jamaica Plank Road (Jamaica Avenue). This view shows one of Brownsville's oldest parts. Some of these buildings were erected prior to 1886, when Powell Street was called Orient Avenue and New Lots was still an independent town. Dean Street is on the right, just past the two trees.

Atlantic Avenue, looking west from the Sackman Street Bridge, 1923

This view shows the Long Island Rail Road emerging from a tunnel at Stone Avenue. Starting at the Flatbush Avenue terminus three miles away, the tracks have already gone through two tunnels as well as an elevated section located between Nostrand and Howard Avenues. The line continued at grade until the East New York station at Williams Place.

Eastern Parkway, looking west at Saratoga Avenue and Sterling Place, 1957

This section of the parkway is only 110 feet wide, 100 feet narrower than the boulevard west of Ralph Avenue. This narrow part approximately parallels the former city line. This section, near the defunct Hunterfly Road, was known as *Keuter's Hook* until the late 1800s. It has also been called Ocean Hill.

North side of Sutter Avenue, looking east from East 98th Street, 1927

Brandt's Stratford Theatre, at the corner of Ralph Avenue, had just been built. Historically part of Flatbush, whose border reached east of Tapscott Street (at the site of the former Hunterfly Road), this section is commonly considered part of Brownsville.

Outdoor Motion Picture Theatre, 1916

The Lincoln Park Airdrome was located on a parcel of land bounded by Eastern Parkway, Buffalo and Ralph Avenues, and Union Street, just east of Lincoln Terrace Park. It was one of many in the borough which became popular in the 1910s. When motion pictures began to replace live theatre in Brooklyn, these outdoor establishments were abandoned and vaudeville houses were converted into movie houses. Most of Brooklyn's movie theatres were built during the 1920s. This view shows the exterior of the abandoned airdrome. The IRT New Lots line would soon come through this property along Portal Street. The house at right is on the south side of Union Street.

St. Johns Place,
looking east from Eastern Parkway toward East New York Avenue, 1929

Canarsie Trolley
- southbound at Rockaway Avenue near Glenmore Avenue, 1917

The old wood-frame buildings date back to the early days of Brownsville. The trolley originated at Hamburg (now Wilson) Avenue in Bushwick and terminated at the Canarsie shore. Glenmore Avenue begins at Rockaway Avenue and continues in an easterly direction through East New York and into Queens. The view of Glenmore Avenue is obstructed by the streetcar. Note the Yiddish signs on the far right storefront which advertise rooms and merchandise auctions.

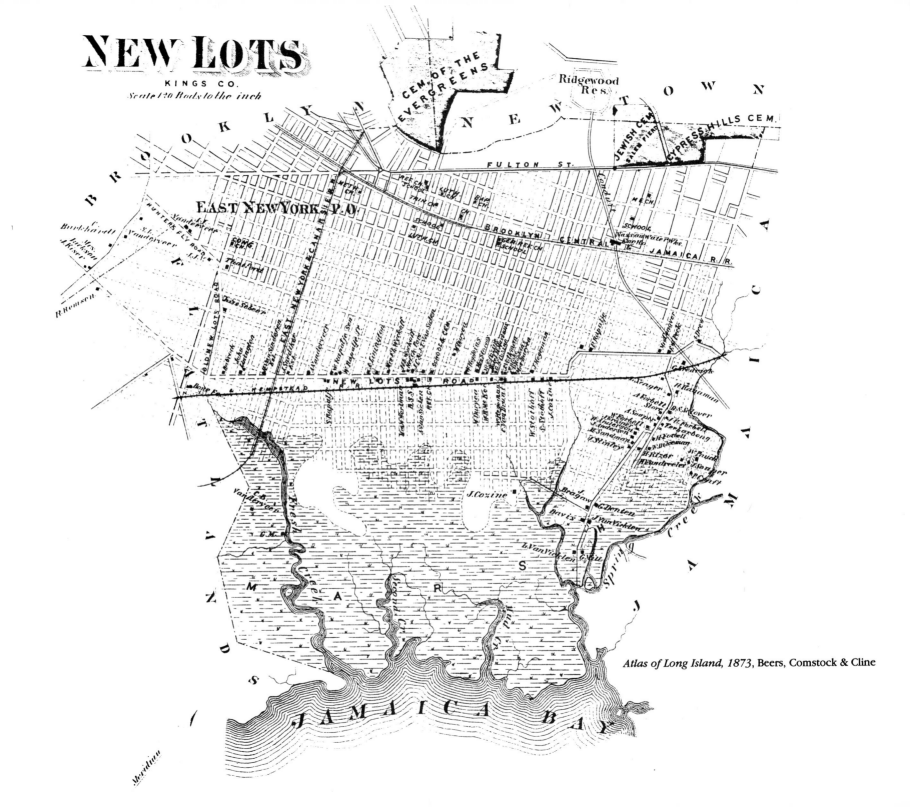

NEW LOTS

KINGS CO.

Scale 120 Rods to the inch

Atlas of Long Island, 1873, Beers, Comstock & Cline

Bushwick

Het Dorp or Bushwick Green, located near Maspeth, Bushwick and Metropolitan Avenues, was the site where Bushwick, one of the six original towns, was established. In 1661, Peter Stuyvesant named the hamlet *Boswijck*, meaning "heavy woods." Many of the early settlers were French Protestants (Huguenots) with names such as Conselyea, Covert, DeBevoise and Devoe. Dutchmen soon followed. The town included all lands north of Division Avenue and Broadway, stretching north and east to the Queens County line, including Greenpoint and Williamsburg.

A dispute, lasting over 100 years, between the towns of Bushwick and Newtown concerned their border. It was finally settled in 1769, when a line was established from today's Highland Park to Arbitration Rock, a boulder now supposedly buried beneath Flushing and Onderdonk Avenues. This line served as the Brooklyn-Queens border until 1925, when a zig-zag border through Ridgewood was agreed upon. It prevented houses from sitting directly on the borough line.

With the advent of "stick construction," a large number of attached frame homes were built in Bushwick during the late 1800s. Ridgewood and Wyckoff Heights were developments consisting of attached brick houses put up between 1900 and the outbreak of World War I. Some of them were built by Henry C. Meyer, whose Germania Real Estate Company also developed Vanderveer Park in Flatlands in the 1890s.

This section had become a popular place for German-Americans. Anti-German sentiment during World War I necessitated changes in some of the streets' names. For example, Hamburg Avenue was renamed Wilson Avenue, in honor of the U.S. President of that era.

Theaters flourished in the Eastern District from 1875 to 1925. George M. Cohan, Mae West and other stars performed at some of the many vaudeville houses around the turn of the century.

Van and Schenck, operators of the Canarsie trolley cars, rose to become star vaudeville players here and overseas. Theaters such as the Amphion, the Grand, the Novelty, the Bushwick, the Gayety and many others provided entertainment for the masses before the advent of motion pictures, radio and television. Many of these theaters were converted into movie houses in the early 1900s.

Bushwick High School, completed in 1911, still stands on Irving Avenue. Bushwick Avenue, once one of the borough's most attractive residential streets, has lost much of its splendor. The area residents, mostly Latino, still maintain the beautiful churches which continue to adorn the neighborhood.

Central Avenue, looking west from Moffatt Street, 1924

An eastbound trolley is passing Lauinger's Hotel on the corner of Cooper Street. Schmitt & Merkel Florists, at left, served the predominantly German-American residents of this area.

German-American social club, 1905

Social clubs played a vital role in the lives of Brooklynites around the turn of the century. Typically, these organizations were segregated by both national origin and gender. Women were usually more closely affiliated with church or literary groups. Here, members of the Arion Bowling Club celebrate Christmas by joining together in song, drinking some beer and knocking down some pins.

Hart Street, looking east toward Hamburg (Wilson) Avenue, 1898

Many wood-frame tenements survive to this day in Bushwick. Young children were often left unattended on Brooklyn's sidewalks.

Bushwick Storage Warehouse
Meserole Street at Bushwick Place, 1923

Political bills endorsing John J. McCusker for Alderman are posted on the wall.

Canarsie

Canarsie lies south of the old Bay Ridge Division of the Long Island Rail Road, on the neck of land between Paerdegat Basin, Ralph Avenue and Fresh Creek Basin. It remained part of Flatlands Township until 1896. The area was named for the *Canarsee*, the tribe which inhabited the westernmost part of Long Island.

The area remained a prairie and marsh until the early 1800s when small houses began to be built along Canarsie Lane. In 1839, Grace Protestant Church was built on that road, now known as East 92nd Street. A cemetery was established off Church Lane in 1843 on lands donated by the town. A year later, Canarsie obtained its own school district, No. 3. Nine Civil War veterans are buried in the Canarsie Cemetery.

In the 1870s, Canarsie witnessed a large influx of Germans. They settled near Conklin Avenue and built a Reformed Church on the corner of East 93rd Street in 1877. A Roman Catholic church, Holy Family, was established in 1880.

In 1865, the Brooklyn and Rockaway Beach Rail Road began operation of steam locomotives from East New York to Canarsie, a distance of 3.5 miles. The purpose of the railroad was to bring passengers to the newly-developed Rockaway resort by way of a ferry connection across Jamaica Bay.

This rail link triggered some development in the area along the shore. It soon took on the air of a summer resort. In 1867, the station just south of Avenue K was called *Holmes*, after the African-American family who lived there. The Holmes family still owns several properties at that same location.

The trains chugged along the narrow corridor between East 95th and East 96th Streets. The railroad service to the shore ceased in 1951, but the right-of-way north of Rockaway Parkway is still used by the LL line.

The opening of Golden City Amusement Park on May 30, 1907, marked the beginning of a new era for Canarsie. Twenty-five thousand people visited the park during its first weekend. Dance halls, hotels and other related businesses opened as the Canarsie shore became the borough's second-biggest resort. More residences and schools were constructed.

By World War I, Italians and Jews had moved to the still-rural area. Three synagogues were established during the 1920s. Ambitious plans to construct a commercial waterfront facility in Jamaica Bay were never realized by its promoters.

Since its beginnings, fishing was a main occupation of Canarsiens. By the 1920s, the waters of the bay had become polluted, and the clamming and fishing industries slowly died out. The result was high unemployment in the area.

The fine pier at the foot of Rockaway Parkway was completed in 1926. A 1934 fire destroyed much of Golden City Amusement Park, and what remained was torn down for the construction of the Belt Parkway in 1939.

Quonset huts along Rockaway Parkway (south of Seaview Avenue) were erected after World War II and provided temporary housing for over 8,000 war veterans. Public housing came to Canarsie in the 1950s. In 1951, the Breukelen Houses opened, followed by the Bay View Houses in 1955. A Long-Island-style development called Seaview Village was built by the Waxman Brothers, Harry and Sidney, east of Rockaway Parkway. In the late 1950s they built about 2,000 houses. The area was quickly losing much of its rural character it managed to keep for so long.

In 1964, three new schools opened, including Canarsie High School, with Carl Cherkis becoming its first principal. South Shore High School opened its doors in 1970.

Today, Canarsie has a strong Italian and Jewish population base. Russians, Israelis and Asians have come to the area in recent decades. Although Black people have resided in Canarsie since its early days, there has been a recent influx of African-Americans into the area, many of whom came from the West Indies in search of a better standard of living.

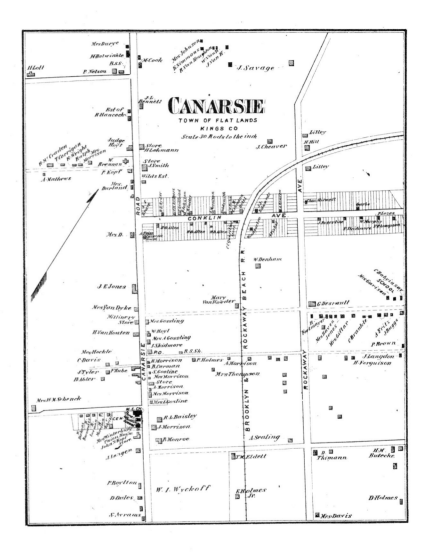

**Golden City Park,
foot of East 93rd Street, 1920**

This resort on the shore of Jamaica Bay opened in 1907. The carousel swing (center) was one of its main attractions. This photograph was taken during the off-season.

**Vanderveer's Mill,
on the bank of Fresh Kill, 1895**

Dominicus Vanderveer erected this tide mill about 1750. His son Charles Boerum Vanderveer operated it until his death in 1879. The surrounding farm and mill were worked until 1905 by John Vanderveer Jr. It remained standing until about 1910. The farmhouse, erected in the 1840s, was moved to its present location at Flatlands Avenue, near East 107th Street. It is now used as a church.

Nicholas Schenck House, 1924

Situated until about 1930 within the confines of today's Seaview Park, this Dutch farmhouse, with its gambrel roof, was built prior to 1758. During the British occupation, the Red Coats set up a guard at this house. In 1897, the farm was sold at public auction. The city purchased much of the land for use as a public park. The house fell into disrepair due to the city's negligence and was dismantled. Part of the Schenck House was reassembled and is on permanent display at the Brooklyn Museum. This photograph shows the Schenck House at the Denton Avenue entrance to the park.

Avenue L, looking east from East 99th Street, 1957

The post-war baby boom drastically increased housing starts in the few remaining undeveloped sections of the borough. This was most evidenced in Flatlands and Canarsie, where hundreds of acres of land were built up during the twenty years after 1945. This photograph shows part of Seaview Village, a 2,000-home development located east of Rockaway Parkway.

Excursion Boats at Canarsie Pier, 1931

The *Albertina* and the *Sea Bird* were two of the many boats which carried passengers across Jamaica Bay to the Rockaways. The completion of the Marine Parkway Bridge in 1935 caused several excursion and ferry companies to go out of business.

**Vacation School - Public School No. 32
Hoyt and President Streets, 1902 (opposite)**
Educational activities were provided for city kids during
the hot summer months.

Cobble Hill

**South Brooklyn Savings Bank - No.
160 Atlantic Avenue, at Clinton Street
(southeast corner), 1922**

The bank was established in 1850. This building
was erected in 1870 on what had been the site of
Jacob Rapelye's house. He was from Newtown,
Queens County, and came to Brooklyn in 1828.
The building was used as a bank until 1923. It was
demolished and replaced with a new building at
Court Street.

Southwest corner of Court Street and Atlantic Avenue, 1922

These early nineteenth-century structures would soon to be demolished to clear the site for the new South Brooklyn Savings Bank. The land still belonged to the estate of Jacob Patchen, who farmed there in 1800. The bank building still occupies the corner.

Nos. 28-36 Third Avenue, 1922

These pre-Civil War frame row houses stood on the west side of Third Avenue. They were soon to be demolished to make way for the YWCA building.

Brooklyn Athenaeum
- northeast corner of Atlantic Avenue and Clinton Street, 1922

Completed in 1853 from funds raised by public subscriptions, this cultural center had its own library and was the site of theatrical productions until the early 1900s. At one time, the Court of Special Sessions convened there. The structure was demolished in 1942.

Program card for Cinderella, ca. 1880

Coney Island

Coney Island was once a large sand bar in the Atlantic Ocean, separated from the rest of Long Island by a creek. It got its name from the *Conijnen* or rabbits which inhabited the island. Part of the Town of Gravesend from 1685 until 1894, the sections of Norton's Point, Sea Gate, Coney Island, Van Siclen, Brighton Beach and Manhattan Beach are all located on a five-mile-long strip. The lands were subdivided into 39 sections in 1677.

A toll bridge may have crossed the creek as early as 1734, but it was not until 1829 that the Gravesend and Coney Island Road and Bridge Company completed the Shell Road. It was built on huge shell heaps and stretched from Gravesend Village to Coney Island, a distance of about one mile. This road is still in use today.

In that same year, the Coney Island House was built, the first in a long line of resorts on the island. The mid-1840s witnessed the construction of the Pavilion, Wykoff's Hotel and the Oceanic, which burned after one season. It was not until after the Civil War that railroad service triggered major land speculation on Coney Island.

When the Brooklyn, Bath and West End Rail Road service began, William A. Engeman, a 28-year-old Civil War veteran, hired a team of genealogists to search for the two or three hundred heirs to the original 39 subdivisions granted to the Gravesend settlers in 1677. Engeman's quest, begun in 1868, was completed within a few years and he was able to acquire title to about half of the island.

By the 1870s, saloons and bath houses began to go up along the shore. By the end of the decade, additional railroads had come to Coney Island – the New York and Sea Beach Rail Road, the Brooklyn, Flatbush and Coney Island Rail Road, which became today's Brighton line, and the Prospect Park and Coney Island Rail Road, which exists today as the Culver line (F train) running along McDonald Avenue. These lines not only ensured the future fate of Coney Island as a great resort, but also promoted the development of farmland along their rights-of-way.

In 1876, Vaux and Olmsted's Ocean Parkway was completed and ran from Prospect Park to the Concourse at Coney Island. This thoroughfare helped Coney Island obtain a sense of legitimacy.

The Children's Aid Society erected a seaside home as well as a sanitarium there, and four grand hotels were put up on the eastern half of the island. William A. Engeman hired the Delaware Bridge Company to construct a magnificent 1,500-foot iron pier. The 300-foot-high observatory used at the Centennial Exhibition in Philadelphia was transported and reassembled at Coney Island, at the expense of railroad magnate Andrew Culver.

The last two decades of the century were boom years for Coney Island as fortunes were made by many who had invested there. Spectacular amusement parks – Sea Lion Park, Steeplechase Park, Dreamland and Luna Park - were all built between 1897 and 1907. Scenic railways and loop-the-loops, predecessors to the roller coasters of today, were built in what Pilat and Ranson called "Sodom by the Sea" in their colorful narrative of Coney Island.

Fires destroyed the great parks not long after they were built, but Steeplechase survived until 1965. Some have speculated that they opted to close instead of integrate their swimming pool. Luna Park closed in August, 1949.

During the early years after 1900, reenactments of great disasters were popular attractions along Surf Avenue. The *Johnston Flood* and the *Ruins of Pompeii* were special crowd pleasers. The Bowery offered dance halls, arcade games, lager beer and numerous other attractions. Freak shows, animal acts and vaudeville drew huge legions of eager patrons. The great bands of the day, including those of John Philip Sousa and Victor Herbert, performed regularly at Manhattan Beach. Widespread gambling and prostitution were included in the carnival atmosphere found on Coney Island.

Coney Island was the site of several famous prize fights, such as Johnson and Jeffries, at the turn of the century. Political corruption led by Gravesend Town Supervisor John Y. McKane made millions for him, but he died a defeated man after serving his prison sentence.

Charles Feltman is credited with inventing the hot dog, but Nathan Handwerker, founder of Nathan's in 1916, sold the most and made the hot dog a veritable gastronomic institution!

Let's not forget the beach! Over a million people could be found there on a hot summer's day. The beach took a beating during the hurricane of 1938 and put parts of Surf Avenue under six feet of water. A terrible Nor'easter did similar damage to the island in 1992.

Sea Gate was begun as a development in 1896 by the Norton's Point Land Company. The Norton's Point Yacht Club was located at the western edge of the island. A railroad shuttle ran along a right-of-way through Coney Island, known as Railroad Avenue until 1952. The line terminated in Sea Gate, near the lighthouse. Today, Sea Gate is a private residential community and is monitored by a private security police force at its two main control gatehouses.

The Wonder Wheel and the Cyclone, built in 1920 and 1928 , respectively, still exhilarate riders. The Parachute Jump, originally the Life Savers' exhibit at the 1939 Flushing World's Fair, was moved to Coney Island after the fair closed. It now stands abandoned – a monument to the island past.

Gargiulo's and Carolina Restaurant still serve Italian dishes, and the boardwalk, dedicated in 1923, still shadows the island's sand. The Half Moon Hotel was famous for the defenestration of the "about-to-sing" Abe Reles of Murder, Inc. It was built in 1927, converted into a nursing home and is now in the process of being demolished.

Alex Silverman, "Mr. Coney Island," no longer sells souvenirs at his boardwalk stand due to his advanced age. Matt Kennedy, now in his nineties, just recently retired from the Coney Island Chamber of Commerce.

The New York Aquarium was built in 1955. The Abe Stark Skating Rink was built in the 1960s, as were the massive housing developments of Trump Village, Luna Park and Warbasse.

The Brighton Beach Baths and Racquet Club may soon become a memory when a new housing development starts construction on that site. Kingsborough Community College, at the eastern tip of Manhattan Beach, was built on the site of the former Sheepshead Bay Military Training Station.

Coney Island today is comprised of diverse ethnic groups Russians, Latinos, African-Americans, Jews and Italians. They live on what was once arguably our nation's most famous playground.

Aerial view of Coney Island's east end, 1929

The Brighton Beach section underwent rapid development after the demolition of the Brighton Beach Hotel in 1923. The boardwalk was completed in that year. At left is the elevated line over Brighton Beach Avenue. Trolley tracks cross Ocean Parkway and proceed along Sea Breeze Avenue. The Brighton Theatre was replaced in the mid-1950s by the Empress Apartments, located at No. 3101 Ocean Parkway. In the distance, Manhattan Beach and part of Sheepshead Bay are visible.

The Oriental Hotel - Manhattan Beach, ca. 1915

Built in 1880 by railroad magnate Austin Corbin, this massive wooden building was the easternmost of Coney Island's grand hotels. The section was known in earlier times as *Sedge Bank*. This structure was demolished in 1916.

Steeplechase Pier,
looking north toward the partially completed boardwalk, 1922

George C. Tilyou's Steeplechase Pavilion was completed in 1908. The boardwalk was completed only up to this point in 1922. The remainder of the boardwalk was extended to Sea Gate in 1923. It was named the Riegelmann Boardwalk, in honor of the borough president at that time.

The Bowery, looking east, 1903

This midway was paved with wooden planks at this time. Dance and music halls, bars and concessions of every description lined its way from Jones Walk on the east to Steeplechase (West 16th Street) on the west.

**Charles Buser's Washington Hotel and Tavern -
northeast corner of Sheepshead Bay Road and West 5th Street, 1915**

The BMT car barn, which stretched over 700 feet along West 5th Street, is partly visible at the far left. At this time, Sheepshead Bay Road extended west to West 5th Street. The area was inhabited by many employees of the amusement businesses, just a few blocks away. It was about this time when Italians and Jews started to displace many of the Irish and Germans in the neighborhood. All of the buildings have since been razed to make way for high-rise apartments. This section was once known as Van Siclen, named after the Dutch family who owned land south of Coney Island Creek. The elevated station of the Culver line (F train) at Neptune Avenue, however, still retains that name.

Cropsey Avenue Drawbridge, 1936

A drawbridge over Coney Island Avenue Creek had existed at West 18th Street since the late 1800s.
As traffic in the area increased, a modern drawbridge was built along Cropsey Avenue's route. This
view is looking east from Coney Island toward Gravesend.

Surf Avenue, looking east at West 6th Street, 1953

Stubbmann's Pavilion, which housed a carousel, dominates this view. Many of the structures would
soon be demolished to make way for the New York Aquarium, now on that site.

**Surf Avenue,
looking west from West 8th Street, 1930**
The famed Cyclone roller coaster dominates this view.

**Surf Avenue,
looking east from West 12th Street, 1930**
The entrance to Luna Park is at the far left.

Balmer's Bathing Pavilion -
east of West 5th Street at the beach, 1893

Originally Mrs. Vanderveer's Bathing Pavilion, and by 1890 known as Doyle's Hotel, this structure was built by Gravesend Supervisor John McKane in the late 1870s for $46,000. The property occupied about 175 feet of ocean frontage and was able to accommodate 500 bathers. Mrs. Vanderveer, born Lucy Devlin in Newfoundland, married William Vanderveer of Newtown, Queens County. After Balmer bought and enlarged the resort, he rejected huge cash offers for it. He died in 1910, and in the great fire of May, 1911, the Pavilion, along with much of Coney Island, was reduced to ashes.

Funeral at Coney Island, 1907

A procession makes its way along Surf Avenue, heading east. The Dreamland tower, with its ornate design, stands proudly at the far left.

Mardi Gras at Coney Island - Labor Day, 1946

This annual parade westward along Surf Avenue was a true festivity. Returning veterans, along with boy scouts, march with flags past the RKO Tilyou Theatre. The Loew's Stillwell Theatre is prominent in the distance.

Schechter Bros. Poultry Store - No. 257 Brighton Beach Avenue, 1935

In a landmark Depression era U.S. Supreme Court case, the four Schechter brothers were able to successfully challenge the National Recovery Act (NRA), when the justices ruled it to be unconstitutional. The Schechters also had locations in the East Flatbush section. The case was still in litigation when this photograph was taken.

Crown Heights

The Crown Heights section, which includes most of Brooklyn's old Ninth Ward, includes the land bounded by Atlantic Avenue to the north, the old Flatbush line to the south (near Montgomery Street), Washington Avenue to the west, and Buffalo Avenue to the east.

The name Crown Heights is derived from Crow Hill, a high point of land along the *terminal moraine* (a geologic feature where scientists say the glaciers terminated, forming a continuous "hill" running from The Narrows, Park Slope, Prospect Park, Crown Heights, Brownsville and Cypress Hills), where an early African-American settlement grew. The old Kings County Penitentiary was located between Rogers and Nostrand Avenues, from President Street south to the old city line. The first road was the Clove Road. It wound through the gap in the hills, beginning at the old Bedford Village, near Bedford Avenue at Fulton Street. It continued between Rogers and New York Avenues, entering Flatbush at Montgomery Street.

The modern development of Crown Heights was not immediately stimulated by the completion of Vaux and Olmsted's Eastern Parkway in 1870. The construction of this 210-foot-wide boulevard raised property values somewhat along its route, but construction of substantial residences did not begin until after 1900. The streets closest to Atlantic Avenue underwent considerable development in the last quarter of the nineteenth century due to their close prox-imity to the fully urbanized areas of Clinton Hill and Fort Greene.

By 1915, most of Crown Heights north of Eastern Parkway had been fully developed. The next 20 years saw the southern half built up. Virtually all of the structures were built of brick and included very large single family homes along President Street and on St. Marks Avenue. During the 1920s, more modest row and semi-detached houses were put up, as well as attractive four- and six-story apartment houses, some quite luxurious by Brooklyn standards. The area along Eastern Parkway had become a first-class residential district. Various institutions, hospitals, schools and places of worship had been erected there.

By the 1960s, a decline in the neighborhood had been averted by the decision of the late Menachem Schneerson, Grand Rabbi of the Lubavitcher hasidim, to remain in Crown Heights. Their colony, which comprises a large portion of the area, is headquartered at No. 770 Eastern Parkway.

The commercial streets of the neighborhood suffered considerable damage as a result of looting during the blackouts of 1965 and 1977. Racially charged violence also plagued the area in the summer of 1991. Recent efforts on the part of community leaders have focused upon bringing the diverse groups together in a spirit of fellowship. Today, most people in the Crown Heights section live peacefully with their neighbors.

Grant Square
- Bedford and Rogers Avenues, looking north from Bergen Street, 1958

The impressive Union League Club at right was completed in 1891 at a cost of $250,000. It was built in a modified Romanesque style and was furnished with its own electric plant consisting of two engines and two dynamos. The bronze equestrian statue of President Grant was unveiled shortly afterward and was sculpted by William Ordway Partridge in his Paris studio.

By the 1950s, the Lubavitcher Yeshiva occupied the building. The Swedish Hospital at left obscures all but the tower and flagpole of the 23rd Regiment Armory (later the 106th Infantry), located between Atlantic Avenue and Pacific Street. Just north of Dean Street on the right, the majestic Imperial Apartments stands.

North Side of Eastern Parkway, looking west toward Franklin Avenue, 1935

A trolley reaches the crest of the hill as it travels southbound toward Flatbush. An outdoor café awaits patrons during the hard times of the Depression.

South side of Eastern Parkway, looking east toward Utica Avenue, 1945
Dubrow's Cafeteria occupied this location for many years until it closed about 1970.

**West side of Bedford Avenue,
looking south from President to Carroll Streets, 1918**
At the far right is the Troop C Armory club house. Ebbets Field is visible down the hill. It was located
at the border of Crown Heights and Flatbush.

Nos. 1048, 1042 and 1038 Union Street, between Franklin and Bedford Avenues, 1918

Attractive four-story apartment houses in this newly developed section drew tenants who wanted to escape the more densely populated areas of the metropolis. At the far left is an old wood-frame house, typical of those that dotted the area prior to 1900. Note the coal truck making a delivery.

Nostrand Avenue, looking north from Pacific Street, 1932

The Long Island Rail Road elevated shadows Atlantic Avenue. Just beyond Atlantic Avenue are the older buildings of Bedford-Stuyvesant.

Utica Avenue, looking south at Prospect Place, 1919
This view is looking up the hill toward Eastern Parkway. Note the advertisements for Coca-Cola and Mazola on the right.

Nos. 1029-1047 President Street, seen from Bedford Avenue, 1919

These attractive brick homes on the north side of President Street had recently been constructed. They are narrow buildings, measuring only 17 feet wide. One third of a mile from the camera is the east wing of the Brooklyn Museum.

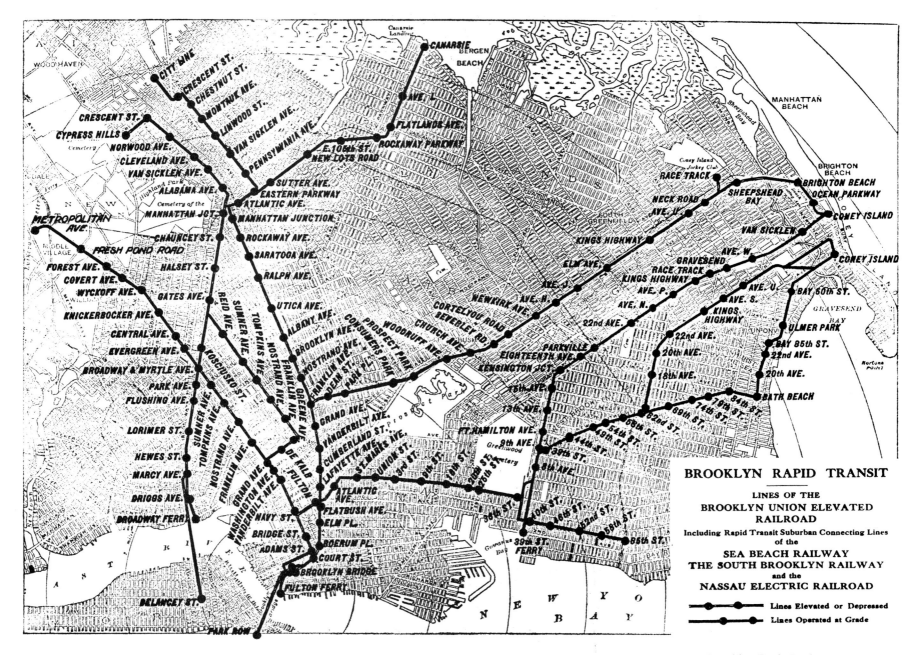

BROOKLYN RAPID TRANSIT

LINES OF THE
**BROOKLYN UNION ELEVATED
RAILROAD**
Including Rapid Transit Suburban Connecting Lines
of the
**SEA BEACH RAILWAY
THE SOUTH BROOKLYN RAILWAY**
and the
NASSAU ELECTRIC RAILROAD

●━━━●━━━● Lines Elevated or Depressed
●━━━●━━━● Lines Operated at Grade

Brooklyn Daily Eagle, ca. 1910

Atlas of the Metropolitan District, 1891 Julius Bien

Downtown

Located on what had been a peninsula between the Gowanus and Wallabout Bays, this section, now situated between the waterfront and Flatbush and Atlantic Avenues, became the nucleus of America's fourth largest city. The area currently includes the shopping district along Fulton Street, the government offices around Borough Hall, Brooklyn Heights and the commercial waterfront area.

Settled in 1640, *Breukelen,* named after its Dutch counterpart, consisted of small wood-frame houses scattered around lower Fulton Street. In 1816, Brooklyn was incorporated as a village and by 1823 had a population of 7,000. In 1834, the City of Brooklyn was established. The Long Island Rail Road was founded that same year. It would soon be capable of transporting passengers and freight to and from points as far away as Suffolk County.

In 1841, the *Brooklyn Daily Eagle*, Brooklyn's most famous tabloid, was first published by I. Van Anden. That decade witnessed the initiation of gas service and the construction of its City Hall. A major fire devastated the young city in the 1840s but with the assistance of the great waves of German and Irish immigrants, the city quickly rebuilt. By 1850, Brooklyn's population swelled to 139,000.

The booming city was also becoming a major industrial center. Factories of all sorts were producing a wide variety of goods. Waterfront activity increased dramatically during these years of economic prosperity. Brooklyn's rapid growth can be directly linked to the progress of the Industrial Revolution.

The Brooklyn Heights residential district, begun in the 1840s, became the first genuine suburb of New York. Fulton Street, Bridge Street and Myrtle Avenue were lined with retail establishments by the close of the Civil War. The section had become a teeming metropolis by 1880.

Congregation Baith Israel, organized in 1854, built Brooklyn's first synagogue in 1862 on the southeast corner of State Street and Boerum Place. That site is today occupied by the Brooklyn House of Detention. The congregation later moved to Carroll Gardens and is known today as the Kane Street Synagogue.

The completion of the Brooklyn Bridge in May, 1883 marked a milestone for the area. As public transportation became available, Brooklynites could travel quickly around the county and beyond. In 1898, Greater New York was formed, and Brooklyn was no longer an independent city. All of Kings County had become one of New York City's five boroughs.

After 1900, Downtown did not stop growing. It continued to flourish as large office buildings were built. The Main Post Office was expanded, and warehouses and factories replaced antiquated structures near the waterfront. Elevated trains, surface trolleys and automobiles soon made Downtown Brooklyn a traffic nightmare.

The Civic Center improvement project was begun around 1940. It involved the demolition of the Fulton Street elevated line and created an open corridor north of Borough Hall and just east of Fulton Street. Cadman Plaza was created to help alleviate some of the congestion in the area. In 1953, the Brooklyn-Queens Expressway project gave birth to a wonderful promenade in Brooklyn Heights. In the process, however, a number of historic buildings were lost. As a result, Brooklyn Heights became New York City's first Historic District in 1965.

Borough Hall, looking from Remsen Street, 1950

This marble building served as Brooklyn's City Hall for fifty years, until 1898. It was designed by Gamaliel King, a Brooklyn resident. The cupola burned in 1895 and was replaced three years later by one made of cast-iron. Recent restoration of this magnificent landmark was completed in 1989. Today, it houses offices of the borough president and other agencies of government.

Times Plaza
- intersection of Fourth and Flatbush Avenues and Hanson Place, 1912

The Atlantic Avenue station of the Fifth Avenue elevated line dominates this view. The Brooklyn terminus of the Long Island Rail Road is partially visible at the far left. It was demolished in the early 1990s.

Fire Department Headquarters - Jay Street, ca. 1915

The designated New York City landmark at right was designed by Frank Freeman in 1892. This view faces north along Jay Street toward Myrtle Avenue where the elevated structure is visible. Horses pulled fire apparatus in Brooklyn until 1922.

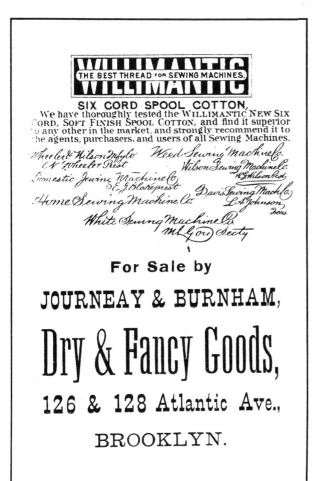

Nos. 124-128 Atlantic Avenue, 1922

This building, located on the south side of Atlantic Avenue, between Henry and Clinton Streets, was once occupied by a dry goods establishment, Journey & Burnham's. In 1922, the Atlantic-Pacific Chandlery Manufacturing Company as well as the Schoen Bros., a women's shoe manufacturer, occupied the building.

View from Borough Hall, looking north, 1935

The statue of Henry Ward Beecher, the noted nineteenth-century abolitionist preacher of the Plymouth Church, is in the foreground. His adultery trial during the 1870s gained the attention of the nation. Many doubts remained even after his acquittal. The Mechanics Bank building on the corner of Montague Street (far left) is now gone. The *Brooklyn Daily Eagle* building (center with tower) has also been razed. The Fulton Street elevated would be dismantled in 1941 and Cadman Plaza would replace most of the area in this photograph.

Fulton Street, looking west from Hanover Place, 1964

Fulton Street has always been Brooklyn's most important shopping strip. By the 1960s, many of the finer shops of a generation earlier had disappeared, and discount or variety stores began to line the street. In the distance are the high-rise office buildings along Court Street.

Flatbush Avenue Extension,
looking northwest from the Fulton Street elevated, 1914

On September 14, 1894, Brooklyn Mayor Schieren formed a committee of five men to investigate and report upon the feasibility of extending Flatbush Avenue from Fulton Street to the East River. The study was undertaken as an attempt to alleviate the congestion along Fulton Street, which was then the only direct thoroughfare leading to the Brooklyn Bridge and the Fulton Ferry. A proposal was adopted which would have connected Flatbush Avenue to the Fulton Ferry in a straight line, but when plans for the Manhattan Bridge were drafted, Flatbush Avenue Extension was laid out to connect to it, instead.

Grand opening of new roadway over Manhattan Bridge, 1931

In response to the increase in vehicular traffic, additional lanes were installed. This ceremony, at the Brooklyn entrance to the bridge, celebrated completion of the project. Note the silhouette of the recently completed Empire State Building in the distance.

Borough Hall Newsstand, 1934

Newsstands were found at almost every subway and el station. The sign on the awning reminded customers to read the *Brooklyn Citizen,* a popular tabloid of the day. In the distance is the Fulton Street elevated. Borough Hall is at left.

Berean Buildings - northwest corner of Court and State Streets, 1922

These handsome stores were built in 1867. Note the early motorized Frederick Loeser & Company delivery truck.

Collision on the Brooklyn Bridge, 1922

Brooklyn bound, a Mack truck crashed into a Graham Avenue trolley destined for Long Island City. The company which manufactures Mack trucks was founded in Brooklyn, but moved west in the early 1900s. Note the advertisement on the trolley for the Republic Theatre which was located at Grand and Keap Streets in Williamsburg.

Wyckoff Street, looking east at Nevins Street, 1918
Roulston's had dozens of locations throughout Brooklyn. Although they were famous for their coffee
and teas, they were all-purpose grocery stores. Note the cat on the roof at the far left.

Court Street, looking south toward Remsen Street, 1924 (following page)
These double-decker buses were purchased by the BMT as an attempt to enter the surface transit
business. The city would not grant the BMT franchises, so the vehicles were sold to the Fifth Avenue
Coach Company of Manhattan. The franchises were eventually awarded in 1930, and within 26 years,
the bus had replaced the trolley in Brooklyn.

Fulton Street, looking west toward Joralemon Street, 1907

The Fulton Street elevated dominates this photograph. Workers prepare to change the switch-track for an eastbound trolley. The Kings County Courthouse and Municipal Building are at left. Note the the women's attire on the left.

Flatbush Avenue, looking southeast at Atlantic Avenue, 1914 (preceding page)

The elevated line above Flatbush Avenue turned onto Fifth Avenue and proceeded to Bay Ridge. Trolley No. 698 passes the Burton Hotel which only served men. Its saloon-style swinging doors are reminiscent of those seen in the wild west. The E.G. Webster & Son Silver Plate Company is at the far left, at No. 622 Atlantic Avenue, corner Fifth Avenue.

Franklin House - No. 1 Fulton Street, at Water Street, southeast corner, 1922

Directly across from the Fulton Ferry, a hotel/tavern known as the Franklin House was built on a 60 by 65 foot lot. This building, as well as the others along the east side of Fulton Street, were erected between 1836 and 1850. The Fulton Ferry area is the only designated historic district of Brooklyn noted for its commercial importance. Note the supports for the Fulton Street elevated at the far right.

13th Avenue, looking southwest to 66th Street, 1934
This part of Brooklyn has not changed much in appearance since the Great Depression.

Dyker Heights

Dyker Heights, formerly part of the Town of New Utrecht, lies between Bay Ridge-Fort Hamilton and Bath Beach-Bensonhurst. It remained mostly farmland until the 1890s when a residential development known as Lefferts Park was begun between 14th and 15th Avenues, from 69th to 75th Streets. Construction in the area continued throughout the early 1900s, and into the building boom of the 1920s. Large homes were built along 11th and 12th Avenues and the intersecting streets above 86th Street.

Today, Dyker's hilly terrain and beautiful homes make the section a very special place. The area boasts a fine public golf course. A strong Italian-American population base has added to this neighborhood's stability.

13th Avenue, looking northeast at 66th Street, 1934

The railroad cut for the Sea Beach line and the Long Island Rail Road is four blocks down the avenue. Note the antiquated gasoline pump at the far left.

East New York

By 1675, almost all the land in Flatbush had been spoken for, and farm prices rose. As a result of the increased demand, Flatbush farmers in search of available land traveled a few miles east and established the "New Lots of Flatbush." The area was located in the southeastern portion of Kings County, extending eastward from Canarsie to the Queens County line, from the highlands on the north to Jamaica Bay on the south. By 1680, a schoolmaster was employed and in 1740 a school was erected on the New Lots Road. The Village of New Lots was centered along the New Lots Road, at Barbey Street, near the Dutch Reformed Church. Today's neighborhoods of East New York, Cypress Hills, City Line and much of Brownsville emerged from what was once New Lots. The Town of New Lots was established in 1852 when it seceded from Flatbush.

East New York was founded in 1835 by John R. Pitkin, a Connecticut Yankee speculator. He purchased a two mile by one mile strip of land near Pennsylvania and Atlantic Avenues and sold lots for $10 to $25 apiece. Almost destroyed by the economic panic of 1837, New Lots, the smallest in size of the county's towns, had become its most populous by 1880. Boasting nearly 14,000 citizens,

BUSCH, BENNER, & CO.,

MANUFACTURERS OF

PANTS AND VESTS,

TURN HALL,

BUTLER AVE., BET. ATLANTIC & LIBERTY,

EAST NEW YORK.

ORDERS PROMPTLY EXECUTED AND ATTENDED TO.

the town's growth was caused by a massive influx of immigrants from Germany.

Cypress Hills is located in the northeastern portion of the area. A toll house once stood at the Jamaica Plank Road, near the county line. Snediker's Hotel, which dated back to the 1840s, formed the nucleus of Cypress Hills. By 1880, the area was home to a brush factory, planing mills and a fireworks factory. Some of the cemeteries north of the Jamaica Road were founded prior to the Civil War.

The Ridgewood Reservoir system of the Brooklyn Water Works was built in the 1850s. Thousands of gallons of water were collected from the inlets along the south shore of Queens County. The water was pumped westward through a giant pipeline which ran beneath today's Conduit Avenue and Sunrise Highway further east. Sunrise Highway was built over the pipeline in 1927. The water was used to supply the residents and factories of Brooklyn until the Croton System from upstate New York was activated in Brooklyn after World War I.

A resort community known as the "Old Mill" was started around the turn of the century. The houses were built on "stilts" near an abandoned mill along the waters of Jamaica Bay, at the foot of Crescent Street. Every year a Mardi Gras celebration was held. The shacks were decorated with hanging lights and American flags. The event was often held on the Fourth of July. The enclave lasted until it was nearly destroyed by the hurricane of 1938. The Belt Parkway construction project cleared away any remnants that may have survived the great storm. A few old timers living south of Linden Boulevard still refer to their section as the "Old Mill."

In 1886, East New York, Cypress Hills and all of the territory which comprised New Lots town was annexed by the City of Brooklyn. Those areas became the city's 26th Ward. Farmers continued to prosper in the area, and cows were visible on dairy farms as late as 1960 in the vicinity of Pennsylvania and Stanley Avenues.

Although Dutch presence in the area remained strong well into the early twentieth century, great numbers of Germans, followed by Irish, Italian and Jewish residents came. They were attracted by the area's fine schools, shops and houses of worship.

Today, East New York is inhabited mostly by African-Americans. Cypress Hills is still well-kept and is a culturally diverse section.

LACKER'S MEAT MARKET,

CORNER ATLANTIC AND BUTLER AVENUES,

EAST NEW YORK.

M ....

....

ALEXI'S Photographic Gallery,

ATLANTIC AVENUE,

Bet. New Jersey and Pennsylvania Avs.

EAST NEW YORK.

Plots, Tomb Stones, Monuments, &c., a Speciality.

North side of Atlantic Avenue, looking west at Georgia Avenue, 1923

This view is looking from under the Long Island Rail Road elevated structure. The tracks proceed to street level at the East New York station, where they then continue underneath the elevated roadway of the Canarsie subway line. Mid-nineteenth-century brick buildings with dormers can still be found in the older parts of East New York.

Snediker Avenue, looking north from New Lots Avenue, 1934

Situated just east of the Brownsville border, where the railroad tracks divide the neighborhoods, this area remained a middle-class Jewish stronghold until the 1960s.

Atlantic Avenue, looking west from Jerome Street, 1944

The industrial building at left was operated by Borden's Milk Company. The Long Island Rail Road tracks had recently been moved underground.

Ridgewood Avenue, looking east at Warwick Street, 1917

These attractive attached brick houses were constructed around 1910 on land which had once belonged to the Isaac Schenck estate. A large brick home would soon be constructed on the corner property (on right), measuring 55 by 100 feet. The ornate wrought-iron fence is indicative of the income level of the district. Part of Jamaica Avenue is visible at the far left.

Pitkin Avenue, looking west from Pennsylvania Avenue, 1929

Pitkin Avenue was named after John R. Pitkin, who founded the village of East New York in 1835.
The wood-frame buildings at left, close to Sheffield Avenue, were built prior to the Civil War.

Highland Boulevard, 1921

Situated on the highest and most attractive part of East New York, these expensive homes still offer their residents unmatched views of the neighborhood.

The Bushwicks Baseball Team, 1928 (opposite)

Just past the borough line, and east of where Franklin K. Lane High School stands today, was Dexter Park. This 10-acre site had been used for recreational purposes since the late 1800s. A modern stadium was constructed in 1922. The park became a profitable attraction. Night baseball was introduced successfully there in 1930, eight years prior to its use at Ebbets Field. Seating 13,500 spectators, it was the largest semi-professional stadium in the country at the time. The great Negro League teams of the day frequently competed at Dexter Park.

The Bushwicks were the team most closely associated with Dexter Park. The team disbanded after the 1951 season, possibly as a result of desegregation in the major leagues. The stadium was demolished in 1956. The club was owned by Max Rosner (in center of photo) and Nat Strong.

Dexter Park, home of the Bushwicks, 1947

This view is looking north from the Jamaica Avenue elevated platform at the Brooklyn-Queens border. Fans are on their way into the stadium to see a game. Part of Franklin K. Lane High School is visible at the left. The Cypress Hills are seen in the distance. Technically, the stadium was located in Woodhaven.

Flatbush

Centered in the heart of Kings County, Flatbush was one of the original six towns. It was bounded by the hills of Brooklyn to the north, New Utrecht to the west and south, and Flatlands to the east and south. The land slopes very gently to the south, creating excellent drainage and soil conditions conducive to productive farming. Until 1852, New Lots, which included East New York, was part of Flatbush. The towns of Gravesend, New Utrecht, Flatlands and Flatbush all converged at a point near East 17th Street and Foster Avenue.

Originally called *Midwout* by its Dutch founders who were granted lands there in 1652, the name Flatbush is an anglicized form of *Vlachte bos*, which means "plain (in the) woods." Part of what later became Flatbush was known as Corlear's Flats. It was purchased from the *Canarsee* Indians in 1635. Flatbush and Flatlands disputed their boundary until 1667 when the border was fixed by arbitration. Well-known names from the area include Caton, Clarkson, Crooke, Ditmas, Lefferts, Lott, Martense and Vanderveer. For a time, Flatbush became the seat of government for Kings County. The Dutch Reformed Church, located at the southwest corner of Church and Flatbush Avenues, has been the site of worship since 1662, although the present building dates from 1796.

The first great battle of the American Revolution took place behind the present location of the Prospect Park Zoo, near the old Flatbush-Brooklyn border. The historic Dongan Oak, designated by the governor as a boundary marker between the two municipalities in 1685, was cut down and thrown across the road by the retreating patriots to block the advance of the British during the Battle of Long Island.

In 1787, Erasmus Hall Academy was opened as a private school. The first public school, P.S. 90, was built on the southwest corner of Church and Bedford Avenues in 1878. That building later served as the Talmudical Academy for Boys (T.A.), and is presently occupied by a girls' yeshiva, Beth Rivka.

By the mid-1800s, most Flatbush residents were farmers or shopkeepers. Attracted by its beauty, businessmen and doctors built large homes along the Avenue, several of which stood until the 1920s. Negro slaves, who had been freed at an early date, lived in a community on the east end of town, close to where Church Avenue meets Kings Highway.

The Flatbush Water Company was established in the late 1800s and dug artesian wells at the Paerdegat, located where the Vanderveer Housing Project now stands, east of Nostrand Avenue on the Flatlands border. The company supplied the area with water into the mid-1900s.

Holy Cross Cemetery was founded in 1849 on 160 acres at Brooklyn and Snyder Avenues. Three years later, Holy Cross Church was established. It was the first Roman Catholic congregation in the town. A large number of Irish families came to Flatbush in the years following the Civil War. They settled in areas east of Flatbush

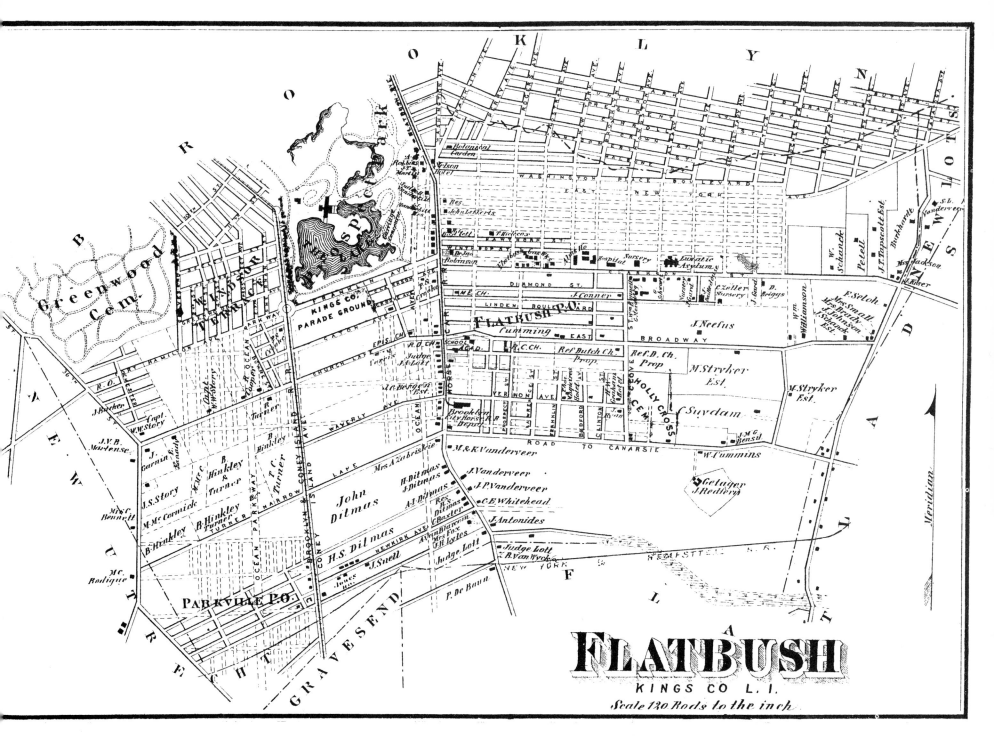

FLATBUSH

KINGS CO L.I.

Scale 120 Rods to the inch

Atlas of Long Island, 1873, Beers, Comstock & Cline

Avenue.

Vanderveer's windmill, erected in 1804, stood near Rogers Avenue at Clarendon Road. Many people took refuge in that four-story structure during the draft riots of 1863. The mill burned down in 1879.

With the completion of Prospect Park, the Parade Grounds, Ocean Parkway, several railroads, and ultimately the Brooklyn Bridge, Flatbush could no longer remain isolated. In 1894, the town had been absorbed into the City of Brooklyn, becoming its 29th Ward.

Victorian Flatbush, as it is known today, came about as a result of suburban home development between 1894 and the early 1910s. In the early 1890s, the Vanderveer farm was purchased and subdivided by the Germania Real Estate Company. Substantial frame homes were erected east of Flatbush Avenue near Clarendon Road and Newkirk Avenue. The company continued to develop farmland to the south, toward the "Junction" in Flatlands and beyond.

Prospect Park South began in 1899 by Dean Alvord. It is the jewel of Flatbush and is one of the premier developments in the entire borough. Its exquisite homes and aromatic gardens are now official historic landmarks.

Rugby, the name given by developers of East Flatbush, was begun

Ocean Parkway Jewish Center
FIRST CONGREGATION OF KENSINGTON
"Tifereth Israel"

550 OCEAN PARKWAY   BROOKLYN, N. Y.

1943

SERVICES TO BE HELD ON

יום כפור   שבת שובה   ראש השנה

OCT 9th   OCT 2nd   SEPT 30th & OCT 1st

FOR THE YEAR 5704-1943

PEW **S** LEFT CENTER   SEAT NO. **8**

PRICE $7.00

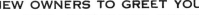

in the late 1890s on the former land of the Schenck family. It was located near the intersection of Church and Utica Avenues. Other districts include Ditmas Park, Prospect-Lefferts Gardens, Albemarle-Kenmore Terrace and Beverly Square East and West.

Greenfield, now Parkville, was founded at about the same time that the Coney Island Plank Road (now Coney Island Avenue) was constructed, in the early 1850s. It is situated north of Foster Avenue, the old boundary with New Utrecht, from 47th Street east toward Coney Island Avenue.

The villages of Windsor Terrace and Kensington, on the western fringes of town, were established after the Civil War, and partially financed by pension funds. Their growth was stimulated by the building of the Culver line along Gravesend (now McDonald) Avenue.

Ebbets Field, home to the legendary Brooklyn Dodgers, was located on the old Brooklyn-Flatbush border. Its demolition signaled the end of an era.

Today, Flatbush is home to many diverse groups. Asians, Caribbeans, Muslims, Hindus and Christians all live there. Jews of many backgrounds, Orthodox, Eastern European and Middle Eastern, live in the areas adjacent to Borough Park and Gravesend. Irish and Italian families continue to constitute a considerable segment of the population.

Utica Avenue, looking east toward the Kouwenhoven farm, 1922

The Flatbush town line extended south to approximately where Glenwood Road meets Utica Avenue. The barn in the distance obscures the Kouwenhoven farmhouse, located on the west side of Kings Highway and within the town of Flatlands. The trestle at left, part of the Long Island Rail Road's Bay Ridge Division, was built in 1908. The Kouwenhoven station of this line was just east of Kings Highway. Sid Gordon's Bowling Alleys occupied the site of the farmland during the 1950s and 1960s.

**Looking north from East New York Avenue at East 98th Street,
toward Union Street and Eastern Parkway, 1916**

Farmers are seen tilling their fields near the border of Brownsville. The New Lots IRT line would soon
emerge from underground along Portal Street, which would be created shortly, at the far left.

Flatbush Town Hall - No. 35 Snyder Avenue, 1877

Flatbush remained a town until 1894, when it became the 29th Ward of Brooklyn. It had been the Kings County seat of government until 1833, the year before Brooklyn incorporated as a city. In 1875, this brick building, designed by John Y. Culyer, was built. After 1894, the structure housed the Magistrates & Municipal Courts. It later served as headquarters of the 67th Police Precinct. Facing the wrecker's ball in the 1970s, it was spared demolition by the efforts of the Flatbush Historical Society. Today, it is protected by its landmark status.

Flatbush Avenue, looking south toward Church Avenue, 1953

The clock on the Dutch Reformed Church reads three o'clock. Students have just ended their day at Erasmus Hall High School and walk home past Garfield's Cafeteria.

Macy's Flatbush - northeast corner Flatbush and Tilden Avenues, 1948

Workers place the finishing touches on the store that would serve Brooklynites for forty years. This building replaced existing three-story storefront structures which were built around 1910. Tilden Avenue was known as Vernon Avenue before 1900. This Macy's store was demolished in the early 1990s.

Erasmus Hall High School, looking south from the tower of the Dutch Reformed Church, 1963   (opposite)

Erasmus Hall High School was founded in 1787 as a private academy. The original building is located in the inner courtyard of the present Gothic style school building. The Astor, Albemarle and Loew's Theatres are visible along the east side of Flatbush Avenue.

South side of East New York Avenue, looking east toward Schenectady Avenue, 1930

Located in the 1860s' subdivision called *Oakland*, this section was adjacent to the Brooklyn city line and stretched from Nostrand to Utica Avenues. Many consider this area a part of Crown Heights. The streets were dotted with small houses built during the 1865-1910 period. Also known as *Pigtown,* its rustic appearance continued until 1925, when large apartment houses and a substantial number of brick row houses were built. Many of the houses from the nineteenth century still serve as residences today. This photograph shows the neighborhood in transition. Note the horse-drawn wagon carrying old rags at Peter Alluto's Junk Shop.

**Utica Avenue,
looking south toward Maple Street, from East New York Avenue, 1929**

The dirt road at left was Earl Street, which was demapped along with Furnald and Webster Streets located further south toward Rutland Road. The intersection of Utica, East New York and Remsen Avenues was widened about this time to facilitate the flow of traffic. The Rugby development of 1900 was centered about a mile away at Church Avenue. Billboards at right partially obstruct views of the Long Island State Hospital and Kings County Hospital. Note the advertisement for the Rugby Theatre at the far left.

Ebbets Field, 1955

Umpires discuss lineups with managers before a game against the Milwaukee Braves on May 1st. The Dodgers won their only World Series that year.

Jackie Robinson, 1947

Jackie Robinson, the first African-American to play major league baseball in the modern era, poses here in his rookie season. While a Dodger, he and his family lived at No. 5224 Tilden Avenue, in East Flatbush.

Ebbets Field - aerial view, 1947
A World Series game is already in progress as taxicabs cause gridlock on Sullivan Street.

East 21st Street, looking south from Regent Place, 1929

Well-kept streets, excellent schools and satisfactory housing attracted people to this fine residential district. Prospect Park is within walking distance.

**North side of Regent Place,
between Flatbush Avenue and East 21st Street, 1929**

Regent Place extends for two blocks, from Ocean to Flatbush Avenues. It was part of the former Waverly Avenue, which once stretched to Coney Island Avenue. This photograph shows Paul Vincent's music school, a Chinese laundry, John's produce store and Chiapetta Bros. shoe repair shop.

Circus in Flatbush - May, 1927

The combined Ringling Bros. and Barnum & Bailey Circ[us] set up its tents on the large lot bounded by Brooklyn, N[ew] York and Clarkson Avenues, and Lenox Road. This vie[w] looking south across Clarkson Avenue, shows the entra[nce] to the side show. Tennis courts were later built on t[he] site.

Parkside Avenue,
looking east from Parade Place, 1956

The author, Brian Merlis, enjoys an autumn day with his father along the southern rim of Prospect Park.

Clarkson Avenue, looking east at Rogers Avenue, 1928

Victorian homes dating from the 1870s have been surrounded by Texaco and Socony gasoline stations. This once-attractive section, located east of Flatbush Avenue, had its older homes demolished and replaced with commercial structures and multi-family dwellings.

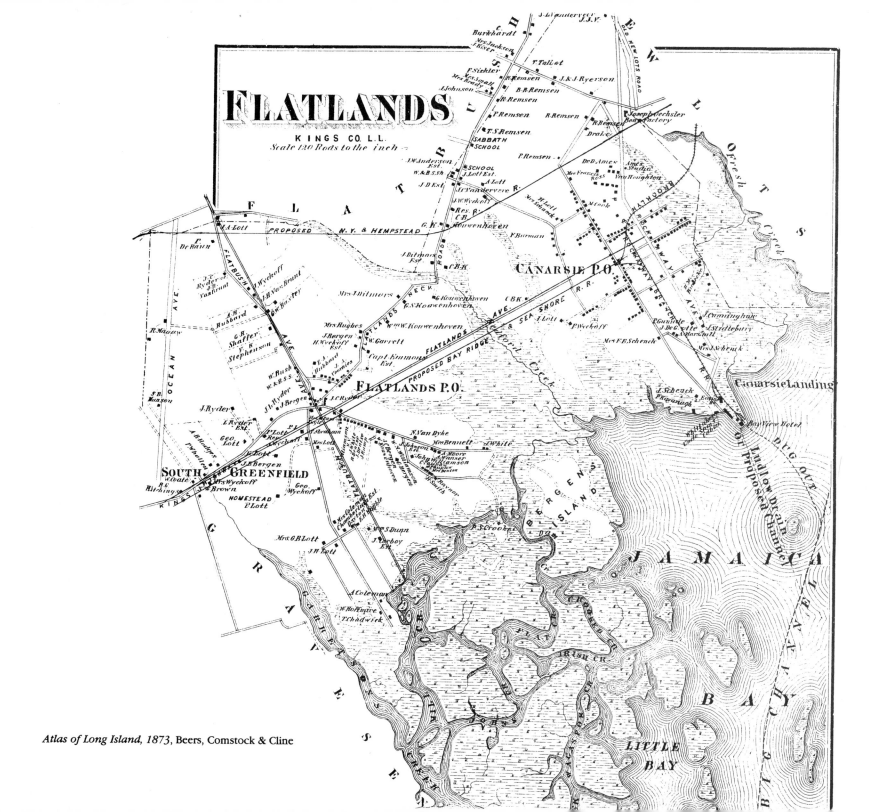

FLATLANDS

KINGS CO. L.L.

Scale 120 Rods to the inch

Atlas of Long Island, 1873, Beers, Comstock & Cline

SOUTH GREENFIELD

FLATLANDS P.O.

CANARSIE P.O.

Canarsie Landing

JAMAICA BAY

LITTLE BAY

BERGENS ISLAND

Flatlands

One of the six original townships in Kings County, Flatlands lies north of Jamaica Bay, south of Flatbush, east of Gravesend and west of New Lots. Originally called *New Amersfoort* after a town in Holland, it may have been settled as early as 1624, which would make Flatlands the site of the first white colony on Long Island. The topography of the area was similar to that of the European lowlands, making it an inviting place for the Dutch pioneers. Numerous inlets and creeks provided excellent irrigation for farming, as well as a source of energy to operate tide mills along the Jamaica Bay shore.

Formal land conveyances by Native Americans were extended to Jacob Van Corlear, Andries Hudde(n) and Wolfert Gerritse Van Kouwenhoven, in 1636. With additional lands acquired by the Dutch West India Company's director-general, Wouter Van Twiller, trading posts were established. Some believe that the Wyckoff House on Canarsie Lane, the state's oldest standing house, may have originally been built as one of those early trading posts. The Wyckoff House was erected around 1640.

The original lands purchased were actually conveyed in rights to three separate prairies or "flats." They were almost totally devoid of trees and were located mostly in today's East Flatbush section, and along the old Flatbush-Flatlands demarcation, near Foster Avenue.

The town's genesis, however, took place further south, near the present Dutch Reformed Church of Flatlands, at Kings Highway. That road, as well as Flatbush Avenue, originated as pre-Columbian trails, and may have intersected at a holy site used for rituals by Native Americans.

The present Flatbush Avenue was straightened in the late 1800s and for many years had been called the Flatbush-Flatlands Turnpike. Its southern branch was Mill Lane, which still exists in a few places. The road split east of Utica Avenue into northern and southern branches, eventually terminating near the Crooke's Mill, at Mill Island.

Kings Highway, east of Flatbush Avenue, had also been called Flatlands Neck Road, Merrick Road and Kouwenhoven Place. It was almost demapped in the 1920s, but was saved from that fate by a powerful city commissioner who, as a child, remembered walks along the winding road dotted with picturesque farmsteads. Instead of becoming a lost piece of history, the road was widened and straightened wherever possible. The project lasted from 1922 until about 1925.

George Washington traveled along this country road on his 1792 tour of Long Island during which he surveyed the agricultural potential of Kings, Queens and Suffolk Counties.

Notable Flatlands families included the Baxters, Kouwenhovens, Lotts, Remsens, Ryders and the Stoothoffs. They tilled the soil for nearly three hundred years.

Barren Island, located in Jamaica Bay, was the site of several industries, beginning in 1845. At one time six fish oil companies were located there. Dead horses were brought to the island where they were processed into glue and phosphate fertilizer. The carcasses were dumped in the adjoining waters, and the name Dead Horse Bay was derived. As early as 1883, many of those factories were connected to their headquarters in Manhattan by a new invention, the telephone.

About 500 men were employed on Barren Island at the height of this industrial period. Most were of Irish descent and established homes, a Catholic church and a district school on the island. The community prospered well into the 1920s. The construction of Marine Park displaced the residents and factories. Many moved into the frame houses which had just been completed in Gerritsen Beach and in the Marine Park section.

Much of Marine Park was built on lands which belonged to the Lott family. The original farmhouse was occupied by the Suydam family, descendants of the Lotts, until the 1980s. The old Dutch farmhouse still stands as an historic reminder at No. 1940 East 36th Street. The house and its three-quarter-acre property, are still on the market as of this date.

Floyd Bennett Field, New York's first municipal airport, was built on Barren Island in 1930. A bridge connecting Barren Island to the Rockaway Peninsula was completed in 1936.

In 1896, Flatlands, the last of the original towns, became Brooklyn's 32nd Ward. The City of Brooklyn had finally become coterminus with Kings County. Residential development was inevitable for the area. The Vanderveer and Amersfort Park areas saw immediate activity prior to consolidation in 1898. Other developments followed along the route of the Bergen Beach trolley, which ran along Flatbush Avenue and Avenue N.

By 1920, the IRT subway had reached the *Junction*, and the lettered avenues were extending in both directions from Flatbush

Avenue. The building boom before the Great Depression consumed most available land in the East 40s, as well as much of Old Mill Basin. After World War II, construction began in the East 50s, to the east of Utica Avenue.

The Futurama Homes, near Avenue J and East 57th Street, were built in the late 1950s. Georgetowne, east of Ralph Avenue and extending to Paerdegat Basin, was begun in the late 1960s. That section is still not completely developed. New Mill Basin, formerly owned by the Atlantic, Gulf & Pacific Company, was built from the late 1950s until the 1960s.

Flatbush Avenue was widened from Utica Avenue to Avenue V to accommodate the increased traffic flow, when Kings Plaza, Brooklyn's only true shopping mall, opened in 1970.

Until about 1970, the Flatlands section remained almost totally a neighborhood inhabited by descendants of Europeans. At about that time, African-Americans, including Haitians and other Caribbeans, began to move into the northern parts of Flatlands, those closest to Flatbush. The peaceful transition continues today, and the neighborhood remains stable. The Irish, Italians and Jews still almost exclusively inhabit the southern half of Flatlands, including the Bergen Beach, Old and New Mill Basin, and Marine Park sections.

Nostrand Avenue, looking north at Flatbush Avenue, 1948

The "Junction" was the business center of the Vanderveer Park area. Just a short distance from Brooklyn College, this area still teems with activity. Passengers await the Green Line bus to the Rockaways. This franchise still links the Queens peninsula with the IRT subway which terminates at the Junction.

Hendrick I. Lott house and farm, 1926

This view is looking north from Avenue T, between East 36th and East 37th Streets. Part of the house was built in 1719 on a farm of 160 acres located east of *Strom Kill* (Gerritsen Creek). The water extended almost to Kings Highway and served as a natural boundary between Flatlands and Gravesend. Much of the Lott property was acquired by the city when Marine Park was created. Almost all of the remaining farmland was sold to developers who built up the Marine Park section in the 1920s and 1930s. Today, this historic home rests on three-quarters of an acre at No. 1940 East 36th Street.

James A. Voorhis House - looking north; Troy Avenue at Kings Highway, 1922

Flatlands boasted many fine examples of architecture prior to its modernization, which began in 1922. Spared during the widening of Kings Highway, this nineteenth-century farmhouse near Avenue K stood until about 1945. In this view, Kings Highway is on the right. Note the extensions to the original structure in the center.

Kings Highway, looking west toward Flatbush Avenue, 1926

Once an ancient trail lined with picturesque homesteads, this road was widened in the mid-1920s, causing the destruction of many historic residences. This view, taken near the center of the old village, shows the service road still unfinished. The Marine Theatre, on the west side of Flatbush Avenue (No. 1952), nears completion on the far left. Brick buildings now stand at the southeast corner of the intersection, once the site of Rem Hegeman's farmhouse.

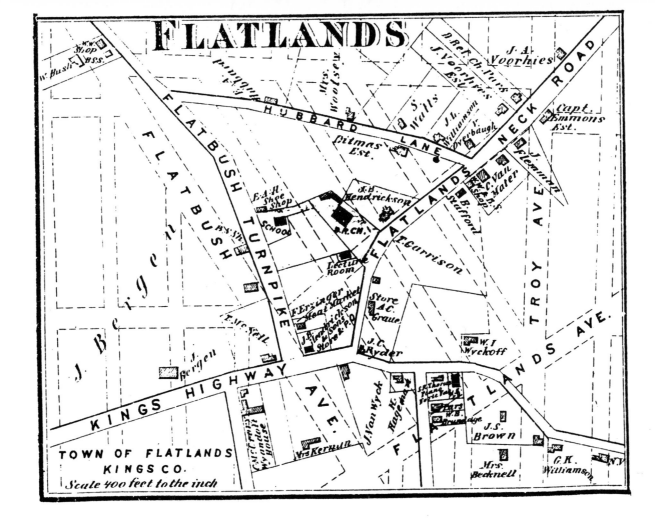

Captain Jan Martense Schenck House - 2133 East 63rd Street, 1930 (opposite)

Today's "New" Mill Basin section was originally an island known in Dutch as *Mollen Eijlantie,* meaning Mill Island. It was purchased from the Canarsie natives by two Gravesenders on May 13, 1664, at about the time that a grist mill was built there. It is generally accepted that the house was constructed between 1652 and 1676 by a seaman, Jan Martense Schenck Van Nydeck. The interior may have been assembled by a ship's carpenter with wooden beams taken from a dismantled ship. Vessels from Holland came into Captain Schenck's wharf during the late 1600s to discharge passengers and cargo.

The Crooke family from Flatbush assumed ownership of the property around 1900, and within a decade, the Atlantic, Gulf and Pacific Company filled in many of the creeks which surrounded the island. The house was occupied until about 1950 by Mr. Austin Bowles and his family. The house was dismantled in 1952 and reassembled at the Brooklyn Museum. The Schenck House was located on the east side of East 63rd Street, between Avenues U and V. In this 1930 photograph, a new roof is being put on the house. Public School No. 236, just north of the house, opened in 1933.

Administration Building
- Floyd Bennett Municipal Airport, 1939

This building was completed in 1931.

Dedication of the Naval Reserve Aviation Base
at the new Floyd Bennett Municipal Airport, 1931   (opposite)

New York City's first municipal airport was named after Admiral Byrd's pilot, Floyd Bennett. The city was under pressure to open an airport because it had lost airmail contracts to Newark, where a major airport had already been in operation. Many historic flights originated here, including Howard Hughes' around-the-world flight in 1938, which set the speed record (three days, 19 hours). "Wrong Way" Corrigan left from this field for California but landed in Ireland in 1938. With the threat of war lurking, the Navy bought the field for $9 million in 1941, although a naval reserve aviation base had already been in operation there for a decade. A helicopter training base was established there in 1943. It was maintained as a naval air station until its closure in 1970. Today, it is part of the Gateway National Recreation Area and also serves as a base for the New York City Police Department's Helicopter Patrol.

Kings Highway, looking east at Mill Lane, 1922

This old house was originally built for the Stoothoff family prior to 1800. Mill Lane extended eastward to Mill Island. Some say that it was a pre-Columbian trail. It still exists at East 56th Street and at Ralph Avenue. Remnants can also be seen in the East 40s, where it had been sold to homeowners whose properties adjoined it. None of the homes in this photograph are extant.

Knickerbocker Ice Company,
looking north across Flatbush Avenue toward East 32nd Street, 1912

A branch of the Knickerbocker Ice Company hugs the sidings of the Long Island Rail Road. The ice house extended back to New York Avenue, a distance of 205 feet. At left is the Hotel Midwood. In the center, just past Avenue H, are homes of the Vanderveer Park development, built by the Germania Real Estate Company in the late 1890s.

Nostrand Avenue, looking north from Avenue N, 1934

All buildings visible in this view were built during the 1920s. The years of prosperity were abruptly halted by the Crash of 1929. This land was owned by George Lott. whose ancestors were major property holders in Flatlands.

James Madison High School - Quentin Road and Bedford Avenue, 1935

Completed in 1927 to accommodate the growing population of the surrounding community, Madison High School is the alma mater of U.S. Supreme Court Justice Ruth Bader Ginsburg.

Fort Greene - Clinton Hill

Located in the area once known as East Brooklyn, this part of the county remained rural until about 1835. After Clinton Avenue had been cut through in 1832, fine homes and villas were built, some generously set back from the sidewalk. Development was slow, owing to the distance the section was from Downtown. By the outbreak of the Civil War, Downtown had expanded, and the nearby Fort Greene section was quickly being built up. Improvements in surface transportation made the Clinton Hill section a five-minute commute from the Court Street area. By 1880, building lots in *The Hill* were not easily found.

A period of mansion construction took place between 1880 and 1910 as the Arbuckles, Bristols, Pfizers, Pratts, Underwoods and other industrialists decided to move into the area. During that same period, great churches and institutions were erected. Pratt Institute, Emmanuel Baptist Church and the Masonic Temple are three examples of that period. An earlier example, the Lafayette Avenue Presbyterian Church, built in the early 1860s, has stained glass windows designed by Louis Comfort Tiffany.

The monument in Fort Greene Park, which honors the thousands of patriots who died on British prison ships anchored in Wallabout Bay, was designed by Stanford White and is the world's tallest free-standing Doric column. Brooklyn's tallest building, the Williams-burgh Savings Bank, located at No. 1 Hanson Place, was completed in 1929. Brooklyn Technical High School, the city's largest, opened its doors in 1933.

Between the World Wars, many mansions were razed, allowing luxury six-story apartment houses to be built. Much of this construction took place on Clinton and Washington Avenues.

Today, Fort Greene - Clinton Hill is an ethnically mixed neighborhood. Its residents take pride in the landmark status bestowed upon their area.

Fulton Street, looking west from Adelphi Street, 1915

The rents paid by merchants were a fraction of what was commanded by landlords a half mile west, in the Downtown district. This is evidenced by the lack of pedestrian traffic.

Williamsburgh Savings Bank
- No. 1 Hanson Place, 1929

Brooklyn's tallest building was designed by Halsey, McCormack & Helmer in 1929. It stands 512 feet high. Its four-faced clock was the world's largest at that time. The observation deck is no longer open to the public. The Atlantic Avenue platform of the Fifth Avenue elevated line is visible in the foreground, along Flatbush Avenue.

Gerritsen Beach

Trolley Conductor, ca. 1900

Gerritsen Beach, 1924

The "old" section of this neighborhood was developed in the early 1920s. The "new" section, a bit further north, was built in the late 1920s.

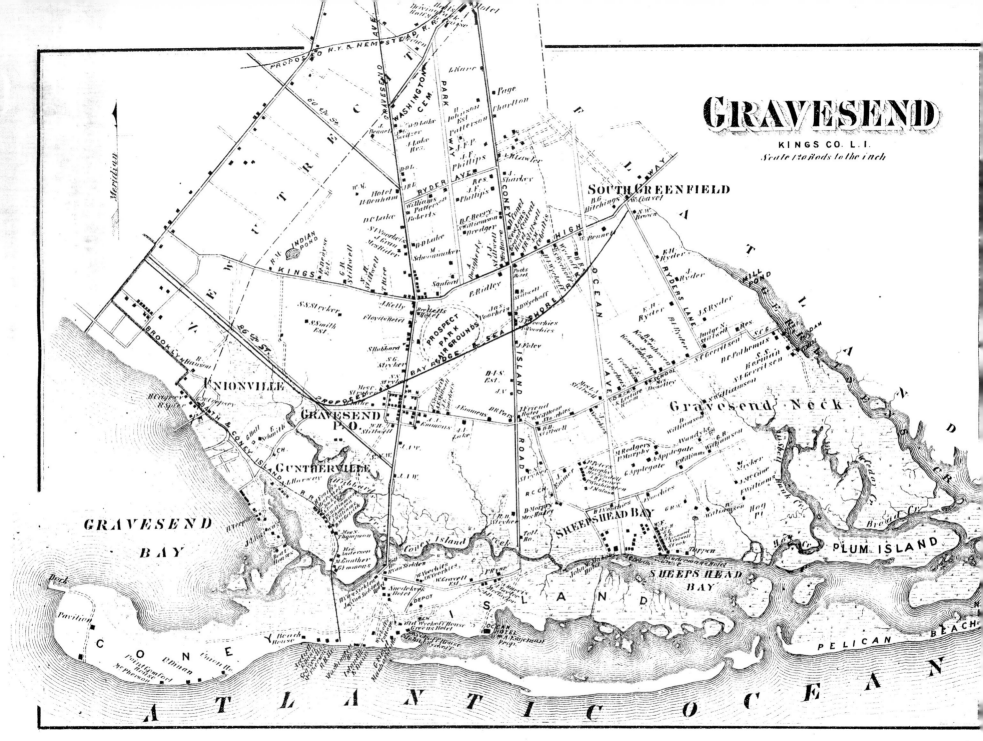

GRAVESEND

KINGS CO. L.I.

Scale 120 Rods to the inch

SOUTH GREENFIELD

Gravesend Neck.

GRAVESEND BAY

UNIONVILLE

GRAVESEND P.O.

GUNTHERVILLE

SHEEPSHEAD BAY

SHEEPSHEAD BAY

PLUM ISLAND

PELICAN BEACH

CONEY ISLAND

ATLANTIC OCEAN

PROSPECT PARK FAIR GROUNDS

Atlas of Long Island, 1873, Beers, Comstock & Cline

Gravesend

Gravesend, the southernmost of the six original towns, was the only one settled by the English. Lady Deborah Moody, its founder, first settled at Lynn, Massachusetts, and joined the Salem Church. An educated woman with strong beliefs, she developed philosophical differences with the church elders at Salem, and was excommunicated. She and a group of followers came to Manhattan and met Nicholas Stillwell, an Englishman. They gained the attention and respect of the Dutch governor of New Amsterdam, William Kieft, and, with the approval of the director-general of the Dutch West India Company, were given unappropriated lands where they established their settlement in 1643.

Wars with the Native Americans during 1643 and 1644 destroyed what had been built, but in 1645 a treaty was reached and the town was granted a patent. Laid out by Lady Moody, the original town square was centered at the intersection of today's McDonald Avenue and Gravesend Neck Road. Four square blocks were planned around that point, and properties beyond those blocks radiated out away from the center of town in all four directions.

Leading families included the Baxters, Bennetts, Hubbards, Emmanses, Ryders and Strykers. They lived in a strictly religious environment. Laws were enacted which forbade the violation of the Sabbath as well as the sale of alcoholic beverages to the natives.

The Kings County Court of Sessions was held at Gravesend from 1668 until 1685.

Lady Moody was a respected advisor to Governor Peter Stuyvesant. He visited her on numerous occasions, and she assisted him in his choices for the appointment of public officials. The woman who may have had the finest library in the entire colony died in 1659. It is still not known if Lady Moody is buried in the Gravesend Cemetery.

A Dutch Reformed Church was organized in the town in 1655. The Dutch and English citizens of Gravesend lived peacefully together, and intermarriage often took place. The relationship between the two groups did not change after the British gained control of the colony in 1664.

A tide mill was erected at an early date at the head of Strom Kill (Gerritsen's Creek), on the Flatlands border. It was burned by arsonists in the 1930s. In 1693, Gravesend was one of the three ports of entry on all of Long Island.

The farming village obtained a post office in 1842. Prior to that date, mail had to be picked up at Flatbush, a considerable distance in those days.

The development of Coney Island affected life in Gravesend. Corrupt officials created a scandalous atmosphere there, and the townspeople had to bear the brunt of much of Coney Island's negative publicity.

Three great racetracks, the Gravesend, the Brighton Beach, and the Sheepshead Bay, which covered 430 acres, made Gravesend a gambler's paradise during the Gay Nineties. The Gravesend Track was dismantled in the 1920s. The Kings Club, a restricted development constructed by Wood, Harmon, and Co., was immediately begun.

The property south of Kings Highway and north of Johnsons Lane (near Avenue U), between Gravesend (today's McDonald) Avenue and Ocean Parkway, was sold off as home sites. Large brick houses, with Spanish-style tile roofs, were built. In recent years, a large well-knit and affluent Sephardic Jewish community settled in these homes.

The Sheepshead Bay Track, located east of Ocean Avenue between Jerome Avenue and Neck Road, had been used for automobile racing in its later days. It was auctioned off as building lots by Harkness in the early 1920s. Large concrete remnants, which once supported its grandstand, were visible on vacant Nostrand Avenue lots until about 1960.

The section along Kings Highway became a major shopping district after World War I. The area felt the full effect of the 1920s' building boom.

Complimentary FOOTBALL

Sat., Oct. 21 - 2:00 P.M. FOOTBALL

Lincoln vs. Midwood • 1961

SATURDAY, OCTOBER 21, 1961 - 2:00 P.M.
At Lincoln Athletic Field
OCEAN PARKWAY and GUIDER BOULEVARD

A part of Bensonhurst, in the vicinity of Stillwell and 23rd Avenues, was within the town limits of Gravesend. It was developed in the 1890s. Resorts in the village of Unionville, located north of Coney Island Creek along Gravesend Bay, became a popular area after the construction of the Brooklyn, Bath and Coney Island Rail Road. The area became known as Gravesend Beach and later Ulmer Park. The resort was famous for its German singing festivals which took place in its beer gardens at the foot of 25th Avenue. Tent cities, hotels, bungalows and boat basins were located where Nellie Bly Park stands today.

Although the Belt Parkway construction eliminated those shorefront retreats, a number of old buildings remain along Cropsey Avenue and along what is left of the old Mill Road, about 100 feet to the northeast. The Cropsey family still owns a considerable amount of property between the Belt Parkway and Gravesend Bay.

Today, Gravesend (west of McDonald Avenue) is primarily inhabited by second- and third-generation Sicilians. A concentration of African-Americans is to be found in the Marlboro Houses near West 13th Street, and constitute a growing segment of the area's population. The Jewish settlement is primarily in the north and east parts of Gravesend. Asians and Latinos have increased in number within the last decade.

FIELD DAYS

POLICE DEPARTMENT
-- CITY OF NEW YORK --

— TWO DAYS —

SATURDAY
AUGUST 21

=1920=

SATURDAY
AUGUST 28

Gravesend Race Track
Gravesend Avenue and Kings
: :: Highway, Brooklyn :: :

Games commence at 1 p. m.

A   97816

POLICE
RELIEF
FUND

This Ticket Good for
Admission on
EITHER DATE

ADMISSION

ONE DOLLAR

No. 95 Gravesend Neck Road
Village Road East, northwest corner, 1930

Dr. Fred E.H. Renaud lived in this house which was erected by J.B. Stillwell in 1860. It was demolished in 1937.

**No. 22 Village Road North
at Van Siclen Street, southeast corner, 1930**

Elly Ryder lived in this house which was erected by J.S. Van Cleef in 1873. The Culver elevated line is visible in the distance, on Gravesend (McDonald) Avenue.

Avenue U, looking east from 86th Street, 1922

This part of Gravesend experienced considerable development in the early 1900s. This was due to the section's close proximity to nearby Coney Island and Bensonhurst. There were, however, large tracts of land available for future improvement.

Coney Island Avenue - looking north toward Avenue Z, 1917

Completed in 1850, Coney Island Avenue was the second road to connect Coney Island to the rest of Kings County. The first road was the Coney Island Causeway, a part of which still exists as today's Shell Road. That road was completed in 1824. Both were toll roads. Coney Island Avenue was originally called Coney Island Plank Road. Its wooden planks were removed during the 1860s when the road was turnpiked. By 1872, the road was widened from 66 to 100 feet. Prior to the completion of Ocean Parkway in 1876, Coney Island Avenue was the fashionable route to Brooklyn's great playground.

The road began at 15th Street (the former Brooklyn city line) and continued in a southerly direction until it bridged Coney Island Creek and finally terminated at Brighton Beach. The section from 15th Street to Park Circle is now known as Prospect Park Southwest. Coney Island Avenue began falling into disrepair toward the late 1800s. As more people began to utilize the modern and attractive Ocean Parkway, Coney Island Avenue was used mainly for the Smith Street surface line.

**Gravesend Neck Road,
looking east from Gravesend (McDonald) Avenue, 1929**

This view was taken from the center of the original village square laid out by Lady Moody in 1645.
The structures all date from the mid-nineteenth century. Gravesend Avenue was renamed McDonald
Avenue after John F. McDonald, in 1933. He was chief Surrogate Court clerk.

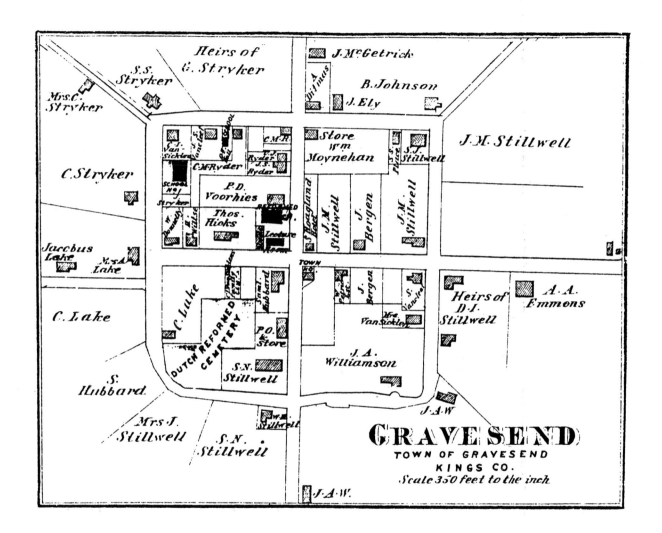

GRAVESEND
TOWN OF GRAVESEND
KINGS CO.
Scale 350 feet to the inch

86th Street, looking northwest from Avenue U, 1930

The West End elevated turns south onto Stillwell Avenue a block ahead. Note the billboard at right promoting Loew's Oriental Theatre.

86th Street, looking southeast toward Avenue U, 1930
The New York Telephone Company building is seen on the left.

Avenue S, looking west from East 17th Street, 1909

Brooklyn Rapid Transit (BRT) cars relax on this recently completed overpass. The Brighton line and the Long Island Rail Road's Manhattan Beach Division ran side by side until the latter ceased passenger service in 1924. After freight service was discontinued in 1935, the steel trestles were dismantled and the right-of-way was sold shortly before World War II. The Brighton line, today's D and Q trains, still operate along this route. Concrete retaining walls from the old Long Island Rail Road are still visible along the east embankments at various points south of Avenue J.

Avenue R, looking east from Ocean Parkway, 1934

Ocean Parkway has also been called Ocean Boulevard or Coney Island Boulevard. The Gravesend Race Track, operated by the Brooklyn Jockey Club, was located west of Ocean Parkway at this point. It was subdivided in 1922 by developer Wood, Harmon & Co. The building at right housed the harness and saddlery establishment of Victor Meyer. It was in business at this site from the late 1800s until after World War II. In the distance, the Brighton line trestle over Avenue R is visible.

Mapleton Park

West End Service Station - No. 6403 New Utrecht Avenue, 1927

Located on the southeast corner of 64th Street, this Socony station sold gasoline for
22¢ per gallon. Part of the West End elevated structure is visible.

62nd Street, looking southeast toward 15th Avenue, 1927

Due to its close proximity to the railroad tracks, this area was zoned for small and medium-sized commercial use. Building contractors, auto repair shops and small factories still occupy this area. A number of private homes also dot 62nd Street.

60th Street, looking northwest toward Bay Parkway, 1926

18th Avenue, looking southwest at 55th Street, 1929

Midwood

Although no part of the Midwood section lies within the old town demarcation of Flatbush, its name is derived from the name of the original settlement called *Midwout*. The area of Midwood includes the northern part of former Gravesend and the western part of what was Flatlands. Midwood is known today as a fine residential section and the home of Brooklyn College, where President Roosevelt laid the cornerstone of the Gymnasium building in 1936.

The neighborhood is bisected by the Brighton Beach line, which runs between East 15th and East 16th Streets. The area near Avenue M was called South Greenfield. The Vitagraph Movie Studios were established there around 1900. A great many silent films were produced there and much footage was shot in the surrounding woods and fields. The company moved to Hollywood in the 1910s, but the studio buildings remained in operation.

In 1925, the Brooklyn studio was purchased by Warner Brothers. A television studio was later built and is now owned and operated by NBC. Some of the productions made at NBC included *Peter Pan, The Mitch Miller Show* and *The Cosby Show*. Part of the old Vitagraph Studios are today occupied by the Shulamith School for Girls.

Wood, Harmon and Company was responsible for much of the suburban development after 1900. The developments of Manhattan Terrace, East Midwood and Nottingham Park went up within the first two decades of this century. Apartment houses were erected, beginning in the 1920s, along Ocean Avenue, Ocean Parkway, Kings Highway and many other parts of Midwood.

Midwood has been a favorite area for Jews since it was developed. The magnificent East Midwood Jewish Center on Ocean Avenue was built in 1926 at a cost of $1 million. Today's Midwood section has developed a rainbow of ethnic and cultural variety and contains peoples from many continents.

Avenue M and Chestnut Avenue, looking east from East 13th Street, 1929

As the newer streets began to take on a dominant role in the area, the original roads of South Greenfield were neglected. The present NBC studio building is seen being built on East 14th Street. The Avenue M station of the Brighton line is visible at the far right.

**Elm Avenue at Avenue M,
looking east toward the Brighton line, 1910**
This movie "still" is from the filming of an unidentified
Vitagraph flick. The building at the right still exists.

**East 14th Street and Locust
Avenue, northwest corner, 1929 (opposite)**
This view of an old house, which had been converted into
a gas station, was taken from the Vitagraph Studio building.
Locust Avenue was part of the original village of South
Greenfield street plan.

North side of Avenue M at East 17th Street, showing Elm Avenue, 1932

A nineteenth-century wooden house stands as a reminder of when this area was called South Greenfield. It was a village located on the Flatlands-Gravesend border. The buildings are on the north side of Elm Avenue. A number of the original streets still exist, as does the Vitagraph chimney, visible at right. The name "Vitagraph" still appears on east side of that smokestack.

East 19th Street, looking north toward the Long Island Rail Road "cut," 1920
The Bay Ridge Division was placed below grade in 1906-07. A newly-built four-story apartment house is visible on the east (right) side of the street, at the corner of Avenue H.

East 16th Street, looking south from Avenue J, 1935

"Manhattan Terrace" was built during the first 15 years of this century. It was a housing development located between Avenues I and K, from East 16th to East 19th Streets. By 1930, the Long Island Rail Road had been removed, leaving only the Brighton tracks. In the distance, the bleachers of P.S.A.L. (also called George Wingate or Midwood) Field are visible, just past Avenue K. The wood-frame homes on the left are no longer extant. On their site stands the new Touro College building.

Midwood High School - Bedford Avenue and Glenwood Road, 1940

This photo shows the school building nearing completion. The name Midwood is an anglicization of the Dutch name for Flatbush which was *Midwout*, meaning "middle woods." Woody Allen is one of the school's famous alumni.

Nos. 1327-1343 Coney Island Avenue, northeast corner of Avenue J, 1925

The buildings near Avenue J on the right have since been refaced and redesigned for use as a savings bank. At the far left is a church which was later the site of a synagogue, Talmud Torah of Flatbush. A man awaits a southbound trolley in the center of Coney Island Avenue as a grocer on the corner passes the time waiting for a customer.

Ocean Avenue, looking north at Avenue J, 1918

Ocean Avenue was completed in 1876 for the relatively inexpensive sum of $15,000. Today, the avenue resembles a canyon formed by apartment houses built after 1920. Note the brick columns at the entrance to the East 20s, on the right. Those columns are still extant.

81st Street, looking southeast at New Utrecht Avenue, 1929

Homes dating from the mid-1800s contrast the four-story apartment houses built in the 1920s, located further down the street toward 18th Avenue.

New Utrecht

John Bennett House - No. 8200 18th Avenue, 1922

This Classical Revival residence was located on the northwest side of 18th Avenue, where 82nd Street was later opened. It was built in 1873. The elevated structure along New Utrecht Avenue is today's West End elevated line.

Park Slope

Park Slope, Brooklyn's largest historic district, stretches from Flatbush Avenue across the entire western rim of Prospect Park. Originally called Prospect Hill, it was a rural area which boasted country homes and villas built in the mid-1800s. The area is famous for its exquisite row houses, churches, institutions and mansions built in the late 1800s. Much of this construction was triggered by the completion of the Brooklyn Bridge in 1883, although some building activity took place in the years following the Civil War.

The area closest to the Park was where many of the wealthier families chose to reside, and a Prospect Park West address is still prestigious. The higher ground was considered cleaner and more healthful by real estate promoters of the day, and those lots would command top dollar. Views of the harbor were also afforded by the higher elevation, along the edge of the park.

Mostly a working class neighborhood until the "brownstone movement" of the 1960s, Park Slope is an ethnically diverse thriving community of artists and professionals.

Grand Army Plaza, looking east toward Eastern Parkway, 1935

The Central Library at right had its foundation laid in 1912. Its completion was delayed and the first floor wasn't completed until 1925. Soon thereafter, the entire $8 million project was scrapped. In 1941, an Art Deco edifice was completed, utilizing the framework of the former structure. The dome, which seems to be above the former library, is actually that of the Brooklyn Museum, located further up along Eastern Parkway.

No. 47 Prospect Park West, 1916
This mansion was located on the northwest corner of First Street and Prospect Park West until the late 1920s.

No. 38 Prospect Park West, 1916
This mansion stood on the southwest corner of Garfield Place and Prospect Park West.

The Montauk Club - No. 25 Eighth Avenue, at Lincoln Place, 1905

Modeled after the *Ca d'Oro*, a Gothic palace on Venice's Grand Canal, this impressive structure was designed by Francis H. Kimball in 1889. Construction was completed in 1891. The total cost for the project, including the land, was $230,000. Membership was limited to five hundred at this prestigious club.

Craig & Brown, Tinsmiths - No. 573 Sixth Avenue, corner 16th Street, 1897
Lower Park Slope was known at this time as South Brooklyn. It was a working-class section inhabited primarily by people of northern European backgrounds. Craftsmen, many in the home maintenance vocation, set up shop shortly after their arrival in America. Their sons usually carried on their fathers' trades.

First Street,
looking southeast at Seventh Avenue, 1922

Park Slope is the largest historic district in Brooklyn. The land on which the buildings in this photograph were erected was at one time owned by Edwin C. Litchfield, a financier whose 1857 villa still stands in Prospect Park. F.W. Walker's real estate office was in the corner store.

Seventh Avenue,
looking southwest from First Street, 1922

The group of buildings at right (Nos. 174-192) were razed in the 1960s to make way for the present Public School No. 321. This shopping strip served the needs of wealthy residents living close to the park. The section has recently become gentrified as artists and professionals have purchased and restored many of the old brownstones.

Kings Court Apartments - Butler Place at Sterling Place, 1916

Apartment houses of this height were uncommon in Brooklyn at this time. Public School No. 9 is located on the right, at the corner of Vanderbilt Avenue. Grand Army Plaza is a short block to the left, down Butler Place.

Prospect Heights

West side of Underhill Avenue, looking north from Sterling Place, 1916

Designed by Shampan & Shampan, Nos. 178 to 198 Underhill Avenue still stand today. A 1924 photograph of the completed stores may be viewed in *Welcome Back to Brooklyn* (p. 133).

Washington Avenue, looking north toward St. Marks Avenue, 1920

Washington Avenue was an important shopping street in the area. This view is looking in the direction of Clinton Hill, past Atlantic Avenue. The A.S. Beck Shoe Store, at right, is on the corner of St. Marks Avenue. An A & P supermarket is at the far left. Note the street vendor on the corner with the umbrella.

**Engine Company No. 219,
at No. 745-747 Dean Street, 1925 (opposite)**

This nineteenth-century building, between Underhill and Vanderbilt Avenues, was on the same block as St. Joseph's R.C. Church (at left).

Prospect Park &
Botanic Gardens

The City of Brooklyn was authorized by the State Legislature to acquire land for public use as a park in 1859. This act was passed as a result of the success of Central Park, in Manhattan. Architects Vaux and Olmsted were commissioned to design the park. They succeeded in making the 526-acre refuge their masterpiece.

Prospect Park is complete with a 75-acre Long Meadow, 60-acre lake, forests, a zoo and rock formations. Bridle paths, intricately designed bridges and an Oriental Pavilion accentuate the park's beauty. Six grand entrances, several with great bronze statues, stand regally to impress its visitors.

The Botanic Gardens, once known as Institute Park, is one of the borough's greatest attractions. Its Greenhouse, Japanese and Rose Gardens, as well as other assorted flora, are treats to the senses.

The subway tunnel between the Prospect Park and the Botanic Garden (originally known as Consumers Park) stations was the site of the worst train disaster in the city's history. On November1, 1918, the Brooklyn Rapid Transit (BRT) motormen went on strike. The management of the company ordered unqualified clerks and dispatchers to "man-the-trains."

The route of the Brighton line started at Park Row, in Manhattan. The train crossed over the Brooklyn Bridge, continued east along the Fulton Street elevated line. At Franklin Avenue the train switched south toward Prospect Park, onto today's Franklin Avenue shuttle line and then continued along today's D and Q lines to the Brighton Beach terminal.

In 1918, a new tunnel (north of the Prospect Park station) was constructed under Flatbush Avenue. It would link service with other lines at Atlantic Avenue and DeKalb Avenue. The junction of the old Franklin Avenue line and the new Brighton tunnel was also being reconstructed.

After Botanic Gardens, the ill-fated southbound train had to negotiate a series of hairpin curves. The signs posted before these dangerous curves read "Maximum Speed - 6 mph!" The motorman of this doomed train was working more than ten hours that day. He was not familiar with the Brighton line route and especially was not familiar with its hairpin curves. He negotiated the very steep and winding Malbone Street tunnel at about 45 mph! The first two cars of the wood-frame train were totally smashed. Ninety seven people died and over 250 people were seriously injured in the disaster.

After this accident, Malbone Street was renamed Empire Boulevard. There is, however, a small fragment of Malbone Street left. It is located just north of Empire Boulevard near New York Avenue.

Litchfield Villa, 1930

Successful businessman Edwin C. Litchfield commissioned Alexander Jackson Davis to design this villa. It was completed in 1857. Its proud owner called it the Grace Hill Estate. In 1859, an act was passed permitting the City of Brooklyn to create a public park. Soon after the Civil War ended, work on the park began. Landscape architect Calvert Vaux wanted the park to extend to Ninth Avenue, rather than to the eastern side of Flatbush Avenue. Unfortunately for Litchfield, his villa was located within the proposed boundaries of the new Prospect Park. The beautiful mansion was saved from demolition. The landmarked building now houses the Parks Department administrative offices.

Botanic Gardens, 1932

The *Euphorbia Splendens* (Crown of Thorns) is being examined by Miss Freda Kane. She tucks in the loose branches to get the effect of a huge crown.

Prospect Park, 1870

Pruning ladder used to trim aging trees.

Botanic Gardens Sundial, 1933

The armillary sphere sundial, a familiar sight in front of the Botanic Gardens' laboratory, was made possible by a bequest from Arthur W. Jenkins. The workers in the photo are seen placing special cement on the ground sphere. The sundial was designed to help visitors locate cardinal directions as well as to calculate the time of day.

Sheepshead Bay

Sheepshead Bay was named after the *sheepshead,* a fish which once flourished in the vicinity of the bay. Located in the southeastern part of the former town of Gravesend, Sheepshead Bay became famous for its fine seafood restaurants along Emmons Avenue, its fishing boats and its racetrack.

Jeremiah Tappen, a New York tavern owner, opened a hotel there in 1845, when the area was still farmland. A small fishing village grew along the shore at about this time. Hotels and restaurants were subsequently built, notably the Osborne House, the Beau Rivage, the Lewis House, Dominck's, Seidel's, Villepigue's, Lundy's and many others. A Methodist church founded in 1844 still serves the community.

Frederick Lundy began selling seafood to the large hotels in the area. After opening a small clam bar near Dooley Street, Lundy expanded and moved his establishment next to the Ocean Avenue footbridge. He entered politics and became the Register of Kings County around the turn of the century. His clam bar expanded, but when the city condemned the property in 1931, the Lundy Brothers built the present Spanish-style building on the north side of Emmons Avenue.

Improvements of the bay began in the early 1900s when dredging was started. By 1913, the water was deep enough to accommodate large boats. Mayor Fiorello La Guardia recommended that Emmons Avenue be widened. Construction of eleven new piers followed in 1934. The two-mile stretch of the Belt Parkway, now known as Lief Ericson Drive, was opened to traffic on May 30, 1941.

By the 1960s, many of the old restaurants had vanished from the area. Large apartment houses had been built along Ocean and Emmons Avenues as well as along Avenue Z. The neighborhood residents, fearing lower property values, established a special zoning district in 1973. After Lundy's Restaurant closed, that structure, along with several acres of his property, was sold to developers in the mid-1980s. That property extended from Ocean to Nostrand Avenues. Since that period, there has been considerable development of residential and commercial buildings along Emmons Avenue.

Sheepshead Bay, 1934   (opposite)

This view was taken from the roof of the Bay View Apartments at the corner of Sheepshead Bay Road and Emmons Avenue. The condition of the waterfront was so crammed with docks, boats, restaurants and other businesses that politicians decided to "clean it up." The Works Progress Administration (WPA) under Roosevelt constructed new bulkheads and, as a result, almost all of the buildings along the south side of Emmons Avenue were removed. By the late 1930s, construction was completed, and the waterfront had been given the clean appearance that it has today.

Construction of new bulkhead at Sheepshead Bay, 1935

The footbridge at East 19th Street connects with Shore Boulevard in the exclusive residential section of Manhattan Beach. In the foreground, workers inspect newly-driven pilings which would soon support the heavy concrete bulkhead.

Looking east along Emmons Avenue from East 23rd Street, 1933

The Lewis House, with its widow's walk, is partially obscured by trees. It stood between Dooley Street and Bedford Avenue. It was replaced with a one-story building and later became a bar called Davy Jones and then Captain Walters. It was demolished in 1990 and replaced with modern condominiums. The area retains much of its Victorian charm.

**The original Lundy Bros. Restaurant
- south side of Emmons Avenue, opposite Ocean Avenue, 1931**
The Lundy family had been in the fish business since the late 1800s. This structure was razed in 1934
to allow new bulkheads to be placed along the waterfront.

Lundy Bros. Restaurant - Emmons and Ocean Avenues, 1938

This view, taken from the footbridge which still spans the bay, looks north toward Emmons Avenue. The tower of St. Marks Church is visible at the far left. Note the trolley car on Emmons Avenue. This unique building, erected in 1934, recently attained landmark status with the help of the Sheepshead Bay Historical Society. Having stood vacant for well over a decade, the structure is presently undergoing complete renovation, and is scheduled to reopen in 1995 under new management.

Tappen's Hotel, northwest corner of East 27th Street and Emmons Avenue, 1923

Sheepshead Bay began as a sleepy fishing village in the town of Gravesend during the decades before the Civil War. Tappen's Hotel was founded in 1845. Tappen;s remained in business for over one hundred years. In 1948, Lundy's purchased the establishment. It was destroyed by fire in May, 1950.

Lewis House - northeast corner Emmons Avenue and East 23rd Street, 1923

This building housed Linderman's Hotel and Grove in 1873. A one-storey brick structure became the new Lewis House in the 1940s. That building became a busy night spot in the 1970s and 1980s as Popeye's, Davy Jones and Captain Walters. It was demolished in the late 1980s. Condominiums now occupy the site.

Emmons Avenue, looking northeast toward East 19th Street, 1923

The Bayside Casino occupied the property between Ocean Avenue and East 19th Street. Part of the 1870s' French Second Empire structure (with tower) was used as part of the Lundy's structure. It was stuccoed to match the rest of the restaurant and its dormers are still recognizable today. The three-story building at left, which had housed the Tamaqua Yacht Club for many years, became the headquarters of the Sheepshead Bay Motor Boat Club in the late 1920s. It was razed shortly before the war. That site was later occupied by Pappas Restaurant and is today the site of the El Greco Diner.

Bayview Hotel - northwest corner Emmons Avenue at Sheepshead Bay Road, 1923

The first apartment house on Emmons Avenue was built on this site in the late 1920s. The six-story Bayview Apartments perpetuates the name of the old hotel pictured here.

Avenue Y,
looking east toward East 18th Street, 1930

The grade crossing of the Manhattan Beach Division of the Long Island Rail Road freight spur, which followed the pre-1907 right-of-way, is visible. A freight car stands on the tracks just north of Avenue Y.

At right is the Permatex Company which utilized the siding. It was demolished in 1991 and a large retail outlet was built on the oversized lot. In the distance at left, the New York Telephone Company's building stands at the corner of Ocean Avenue. The planks on the left rest on the property of the Brighton Lumber & Trim Company, now the site of Doody's Store.

Gravesend Neck Road, looking east from East 19th Street toward Ocean Avenue, 1922

Neck Road continued all the way to Gerritsen Avenue in the 1920s. Today, it extends only to Nostrand Avenue near Avenue U. *Gravesend Neck* refers to the land located in the extreme southeast corner of the township, located approximately between today's Nostrand Avenue and Gerritsen's Creek.

Shore Boulevard, looking southeast from Emmons Avenue, ca. 1911

This section of Shore Boulevard was built as a bridge on landfill across Coney Island Creek, whose waters met at Sheepshead Bay at about this point. In the distance, the Manhattan Beach Hotel is visible. Part of the Oriental Hotel is seen to the far left. The waters of Sheepshead Bay now terminate at this point, and a small park there was named Holocaust Memorial Mall in the 1980s.

South Brooklyn

The City of Brooklyn had its origins in 1636 when William Bennett and Jacques Bentyn purchased 930 acres at Gowanus from the Native Americans. The area is believed to have gotten its name from *Gowane*, a Mohawk, who lived in the vicinity. It wasn't until about 1640 that a ferry was established near the Heights and the section around Fulton Street was settled.

The name South Brooklyn refers to the old City of Brooklyn, when this section was its southernmost part. South Brooklyn remained rural until 1836, when ferry service from Manhattan to Atlantic Avenue commenced. The areas known as Boerum Hill and Cobble Hill became centers of active land speculation and construction from 1835 until the late 1850s. Much of this activity took place on the streets immediately south of Atlantic Avenue. When the Hamilton Ferry service began in 1846, construction began in Carroll Gardens. Considerable speculation was stimulated by the opening of Green-Wood Cemetery. Hamilton Ferry followed the approximate path of today's Brooklyn-Battery Tunnel, and provided a faster route for New Yorkers traveling to Green-Wood.

By 1880, almost all of the section between Hamilton and Atlantic Avenues, west of Nevins Street, was built up. Winston Churchill's mother, Jenny Jerome, was born at No. 197 Amity Street in 1854. Her father, Leonard, was one of the founders of the Coney Island Jockey Club. Horse races of that club took place at the Sheepshead Bay Track. Jerome Avenue in Sheepshead Bay, as well as in The Bronx, are named after him.

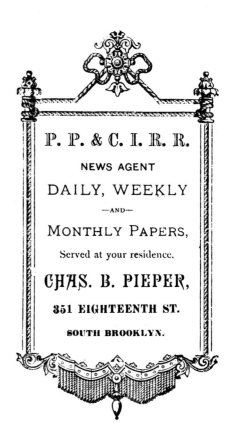

Some of the borough's most unique architectural treasures are preserved in this section. The Home and Tower Model Tenements, built in the late 1870s on Hicks Street, were financed by Alfred Tredway White as a challenge to accommodate working-class people in high-quality apartments. Warren Place includes thirty-four houses, each measuring only eleven feet wide. This street is one of Brooklyn's most charming.

Washington Park Baseball Grounds, located on the former site of Denton's Mill Pond at 4th Avenue and 3rd Street, was home to the Brooklyn baseball team from the late 1890s until Ebbets Field was completed in 1913. The stadium survived until the mid 1920s.

South Brooklyn has been home to a variety of manufacturing concerns over the years, and its industrial importance continues to this day. Two huge waterfront complexes, the Atlantic and Erie Basins, were built in the 1840s and 1850s, respectively. Bush Terminal was constructed in the early 1900s. Major rail facilities had been installed to accommodate the huge amount of freight transported in and around the wharves and docks of South Brooklyn. In 1950, a great vehicular tunnel, the Brooklyn-Battery Tunnel, linking Brooklyn to Manhattan, was completed.

Today, South Brooklyn's real estate values are among the borough's highest. Gentrified in recent decades, this area maintains a diverse population base. Still, second and third generation Italians are the majority near the intersection of Court and President Streets.

terior of Flaherty's Café - No. 1 West
h Street, at Smith Street (northeast
rner), 1915   (opposite)

is saloon, with its swinging doors and beer
rrels on the floor, was typical of what existed in
ooklyn prior to Prohibition. When the
nendment was repealed, more modern "gin
lls" were built throughout the borough. There is
other West 9th Street in Brooklyn, in the
avesend section.

Fazio China and Glassware Corporation Truck, ca. 1937

**Tugboat *Bay Ridge*
on Gowanus Canal, looking east, 1925**
With the coal yards of Greason & Dalzell visible off Third
Street and Second Avenue, the tugboat rests anchored on
the murky waters of the Gowanus Canal.

Gowanus Canal, 1934   (opposite)
Heavy traffic, mostly produced by coal barges, conges
the canal. The concrete-encased steel trestle is part of t
Independent subway line (F & G trains).

Sunset Park

Situated between Green-Wood Cemetery and 60th Street, and stretching from New York Bay to about 7th Avenue, Sunset Park comprised the southernmost part of the City of Brooklyn until 1898, and was known as the 8th Ward. Its remote location delayed its development until Finnish immigrants settled and built homes there during the late nineteenth century. New York's first co-operative apartments were established there by Finns around 1900, at 816-826 43rd Street. Other Scandinavians, Germans and Irish moved to Sunset Park about the same time.

By 1925, the Sunset Park section was almost totally built up. The neighborhood is named for the 25-acre park situated in the area. Notable for Our Lady of Perpetual Help, the borough's largest church, Sunset Park boasts many intact rows of beautifully maintained brownstones. Today a favorite with Asian-Americans and Latinos, Sunset Park is still home to many "old-timers" of northern European ancestry.

**Fifth Avenue,
looking northeast at 58th Street, 1918 (opposite)**
The main shopping district in the neighborhood had many
fine stores.

49th Street, looking northwest at Sixth Avenue, 1925
This working-class neighborhood was considered part of South Brooklyn until consolidation in 1898.
Development in the latter part of the nineteenth century was accelerated by an influx of immigrants
from Finland. By the early 1900s, most of this section had been built up with stores, row houses of
many types and small apartment houses.

Williamsburg

Purchased from the Native Americans on August 1, 1638 by the Dutch West India Company, the land along the East River was incorporated as part of the original Town of Bushwick in 1661. Although primarily creeks and mud flats, farmers plowed its arable sections. In 1792, a speculator, Richard M. Woodhull, acquired 13 acres of land near the present North 2nd Street from the Titus family. Col. Jonathan Williams, a U.S. engineer, surveyed the property, and Woodhull named the new settlement *Williamsburgh*, in his honor.

The first speculation failed, as well as a second development known as *Yorkton*, but a ferry and tavern were established along the shore. Growth was slow, but finally in 1827 *Williamsburgh* officially became a village, a status it maintained until 1851. A Hook & Ladder was operating in 1829. That same year saw the establishment of a Post Office, with Lewis Sanford becoming the village's Postmaster. The population at that time surpassed one thousand.

The 1830s saw a boom and bust as wealthy New Yorkers such as Horace Greeley invested heavily in the growing suburb. The Panic of 1837 was a great setback for the village and recovery didn't occur until 1844. By the late 1840s there was growth of industry in the area, and by 1852 the thriving village attained city status.

FALL OF A DWELLING HOUSE, WILLIAMSBURGH, L. I.

In 1855, partly as a result of mounting debts, *Williamsburgh,* as well as Greenpoint and the remaining lands in the Town of Bushwick were annexed by the rapidly growing City of Brooklyn. Division Avenue had been the boundary between the two cities. The annexed areas became designated as the Eastern District of Brooklyn (Brooklyn, E.D.) until the formation of Greater New York in 1898. Those 43 years coincided with a phenomenal growth as the section became an industrial, cultural and residential center. It was during this period that the "h" in *Williamsburgh* was dropped.

The completion of the Williamsburg Bridge in 1903 marked a milestone for the community as the way was opened for thousands of people who flocked across the river from the crowded tenements of Manhattan. Trolley service over the crossing was initiated in 1905 and Italians, Jews, Poles and other immigrants made Williamsburg and other parts of the borough their new home. Commencement of elevated train service over the bridge in 1905 increased the pace of this mass exodus.

Industry flourished as Williamsburg became a vital part of the great metropolis. By the 1920s the section was densely populated, and the demography had shifted from Anglo-German to mainly "new immigrants," predominantly from Eastern Europe. The World Wars boosted industrial production, and businesses which supplied the nearby Navy Yard prospered. After World War II, the children who had been raised during the previous 30 years had begun to move out.

The fine educational system of that day had enabled many in that generation to advance themselves into positions of responsibility in the public as well as in the private sector. They moved and raised their families in newly developed sections of Brooklyn and elsewhere.

The neighborhood was divided by the construction of the Brooklyn-Queens Expressway in the 1950s. Those years witnessed the condemnation of nineteenth-century homes as public housing went up around the area.

Latinos, mostly from Puerto Rico, have lived in Williamsburg since the early 1900s. A great migration of Latinos shifted the character of the district. The majority of the Jewish population in Williamsburg today consists of the ultra-Orthodox hasidim. They arrived as Holocaust survivors following World War II.

A pocket of Italians still prospers around Lorimer Street. Recent arrivals from Poland and the old Communist Bloc nations live on the *northside*, near the Greenpoint border. In recent years, artists have colonized a section of lofts along Kent Avenue near Broadway at the waterfront.

Williamsburg, like much of Brooklyn, has been shaped by the comings and goings of different groups trying to fulfill their American dream.

Williamsburg Plaza, Brooklyn, N.Y.

Williamsburg Bridge Plaza, 1906

This seven-acre plaza opened with the completion of the Williamsburg Bridge in December, 1903. Known also as Washington Plaza, this area became the business and transportation hub of the Eastern District. The domed white building on the left is the Williamsburg Trust Company. The dark building with columns , toward the right, is the First Presbyterian Church, erected in 1848. The steeple in the center belongs to the South Third Street Presbyterian Church, located on the corner of Driggs Avenue. It was completed in 1846.

Public School No. 16 - Wilson Street near Bedford Avenue, 1931

This famous school was erected in 1858. During the Civil War, it served as a hospital for Union wounded.

Trolley terminus at Williamsburg Bridge Plaza, 1921
A lone patrolman stands on Roebling Street on an April day. Piles of cobblestone await replacement.

Bedford Avenue, looking south toward South 6th Street and Broadway, 1921

This view of Bedford Avenue was taken from beneath the roadway of the Williamsburg Bridge. To the far right is the Nassau branch of the Mechanics' Bank, past the Broadway elevated. The automobile is parked next to the landmark Kings County Savings Bank, located at No. 135 Broadway. It was designed by King & Wilcox in 1868.

Farber's Kosher Meats - No. 99 Lee Avenue, 1935

Abraham Farber and his son Max pose for the photographer. The elder Farber (1874-1957) emigrated from Odessa in 1904 and worked as a butcher for over fifty years. Abraham Farber's daughter, Rose, is the author's paternal grandmother.

oungerman's Kosher
erman Delicatessen - No. 385 Marcy
venue at Middleton Street, 1918

he kosher delicatessen, a quickly disappearing
ght on Brooklyn's landscape, evolved from
erman-American establishments such as
oungerman's. Visible in the reflection on the
indow are buildings along the east side of Marcy
venue, looking north toward Lynch and Heyward
treets.

Trolley Turntable, 1921

This view is looking east along the south side of the Williamsburg Bridge, toward Bedford Avenue.

New York & Brooklyn Casket Company
Bedford Avenue at Lynch and Wallabout Streets, 1920

Located just one quarter mile east of the Brooklyn Navy Yard, this factory was in a section dominated by lumber yards. The delivery vehicles had the capacity to transport coffins all around town. This company also had a branch at No. 503 Atlantic Avenue.

Wallabout Market, 1940

This market was established in 1884 by the City of Brooklyn on land leased from the Federal government on the Navy Yard Reservation. Located on the Wallabout Bay just east of the Navy Yard, it had a wharf as well as railroad access. When the marketplace proved successful, the city was able to acquire the land from Washington. By 1900, businesses in the market had total gross sales of $25 million, and rents paid by merchants made money for the city. Farmers from Kings County, as well as from other parts of Long Island, were able to enter the area for a fee and thus offer their produce to the wholesalers. When World War II began, the city tore down the old marketplace in order to expand the Navy Yard's production capacity for the war effort. Shortly after the war ended, a new terminal market was built in the Canarsie section.

Catalog

Israelowitz Publishing

P.O.Box 228 Brooklyn, NY 11229

Tel. (718) 951-7072   FAX (718) 951-7072

GUIDE TO JEWISH EUROPE - Western Europe 9th Edition by Oscar Israelowitz
354 pages (paper) ISBN 1-878741-19-5 **$14.95** (plus $2.50 shipping)

ITALY JEWISH TRAVEL GUIDE by Annie Sacerdoti
242 pages (paper) ISBN 1-8787-15-2 **$14.95** (plus $2.50 shipping)

THE BEST JEWISH TRAVEL GUIDE TO ISRAEL by Asher Israelowitz
351 pages (paper) ISBN 1-878741-18-7 **$19.95** (plus $3.00 shipping)

THE COMPLETE UNITED STATES JEWISH TRAVEL GUIDE - Third Edition
by Oscar Israelowitz   450 pages (paper) ISBN 1-878741-23-3 **$14.95** (plus $3.00 shipping)

EAT YOUR WAY THROUGH AMERICA - A Kosher Dining Guide (1995 Edition)
by Oscar Israelowitz 126 pages (paper) ISBN 1-878741-22-5 **$6.95** (plus $2.00 Shipping)

CANADA JEWISH TRAVEL GUIDE by Oscar Israelowitz
196 pages (paper) ISBN 1-878741-10-1 **$9.95** (plus $2.00 shipping)

U.S. HOLOCAUST MEMORIAL MUSEUM & WASHINGTON, D.C. GUIDE
by Oscar Israelowitz   126 pages (paper) ISBN 1-878741-16-0 **$7.95** (plus $2.00 shipping)

GUIDE TO THE JEWISH WEST by Oscar Israelowitz
320 pages (paper) ISBN 1-878741-06-3 **$11.95** (plus $2.50 shipping)

SYNAGOGUES OF THE UNITED STATES by Oscar Israelowitz
200 pages (paper) ISBN 1-878741-09-8 **$24.95** (plus $3.00 shipping)
       (hard cover) ISBN 1-878741-11-X **$29.95** (plus $4.00 shipping)

WELCOME BACK TO BROOKLYN by Brian Merlis & Oscar Israelowitz
172 pages (paper) ISBN 1-878741-14-4 **$19.95** (plus $3.00 shipping)

BROOKLYN - THE WAY IT WAS by Brian Merlis
250 pages (paper) ISBN 1-878741-20-9 **$24.95** (plus $3.00 shipping)
(hard cover) ISBN 1-878741-21-7 **$39.95** (plus $4.00 shipping)

EARLY VIEWS OF BOROUGH PARK by Oscar Israelowitz
95 pages (paper) ISBN 1-878741-12-8 **$4.95** (plus $2.00 shipping)

FLATBUSH GUIDE by Oscar Israelowitz
126 pages (paper) ISBN 0-9611036-9-8 **$4.95** (plus $2.00 shipping)

CATSKILLS GUIDE by Oscar Israelowitz
126 pages (paper) ISBN 1-878741-07-1 **$4.95** (plus $2.00 shipping)

NEW YORK CITY SUBWAY GUIDE by Oscar Israelowitz
260 pages (paper) ISBN 0-9611036-7-1 **$6.95** (plus $2.50 shipping)

ELLIS ISLAND GUIDE with Lower Manhattan by Oscar Israelowitz
126 pages (paper) ISBN 1-878741-01-2 **$7.95** (plus $2.00 shipping)

LOWER EAST SIDE GUIDE - 4th Edition by Oscar Israelowitz
126 pages (paper) ISBN 1-878741-04-7 **$6.95** (plus $2.00 shipping)

NEW YORK CITY JEWISH TRAVEL GUIDE by Oscar Israelowitz
196 pages (paper) ISBN 1-878741-17-9 **$11.95** (plus $2.50 shipping)

GUIDE TO JEWISH U.S.A. Volume II - The South by Oscar Israelowitz
175 pages (paper) ISBN 0-9611036-6-3 **$9.95** (plus $2.00 shipping)

Index

"Your Bridge   *to the Past"*

BROOKLYN COLLECTIBLES

TRADER IN ANTIQUE ITEMS RELATED TO THE HISTORIES OF KINGS, QUEENS,
NASSAU & SUFFOLK COUNTIES AS WELL AS NEW YORK CITY & ITS ENVIRONS

n Merlis, Proprietor

-593-4505

68 Westminster Road
Lynbrook, NY 11563

s • LIRR • books • medals • prints • relics • badges • plates • objects • atlases • tickets • buttons • ribbons • artwork • politics • ephemera
venirs • brochures • negatives • genealogy • histories • viewbooks • documents • paintings • billheads • broadsides • scrapbooks • handbills
t cards • newspapers • autographs • timetables • letterheads • advertising • photographs • Long Island • Dodger items • business cards
stock certificates • transportation • trade cards, &c.

TORICAL RESEARCH DONE   HISTORICAL PHOTOGRAPHS PROVIDED